Design and Construction

'At 1 p.m. the 68-pounder carronade on the larboard side of Victory's *forecastle, containing its customary charge of one round shot and a keg filled with 500 musket balls, was fired right into the cabin windows of the* Bucentaure. *As the* Victory *slowly moved a-head, every gun of the remaining 50 upon her broadside, all double, and some treble shotted, was deliberately discharged in the same raking manner. So close were the ships, that the larboard main-arm of the British three-decker, as she rolled, touched the vangs of her opponent's gaff: so close indeed, that had there been wind enough to blow it out, the French ensign trailing at the* Bucentaure's *peak might, even at this early period of the action, have been a trophy in the hands of* Victory's *crew. While listening, with the characteristic avidity, to the deafening crash made by their shot in the French ship's hull, the British crew nearly suffocated with the clouds of black smoke that entered the* Victory's *port holes; and Lord Nelson, Captain Hardy, and others that were walking the quarterdeck, had their clothes covered with the dust which issued from the crumbled wood-work of the* Bucentaure's *stern…"* [Quoted from 'The Battle of Trafalgar: A History' by Sir Harris Nicholas, in *The Despatches and Letters of Lord Nelson*, Volume VII, Henry Coburn, 1846]

Victory and Nelson will forever be entwined but *Victory* had a long history before the Battle of Trafalgar and long history afterwards. She served as the flagship for several illustrious Admirals, including Hyde Parker, Richard Kempenfelt, Richard Howe, and John Jervis who all favoured *Victory* for her fine sailing qualities and for the weight of metal she could throw at the enemy. Unlike many First Rate vessels carrying 100 guns or more that pushed their way through the water, *Victory* cut her way even in the

Victory going down-Channel in 1793 in a painting by Monamy Swaine. At the time she was flagship of Lord Hood, Vice Admiral of the Red (his red flag is flying from the fore mast) and was outward-bound to take command of the Mediterranean Fleet. It is a convincing portrait of the ship's appearance at the time. *(© National Maritime Museum, London BHC3696)*

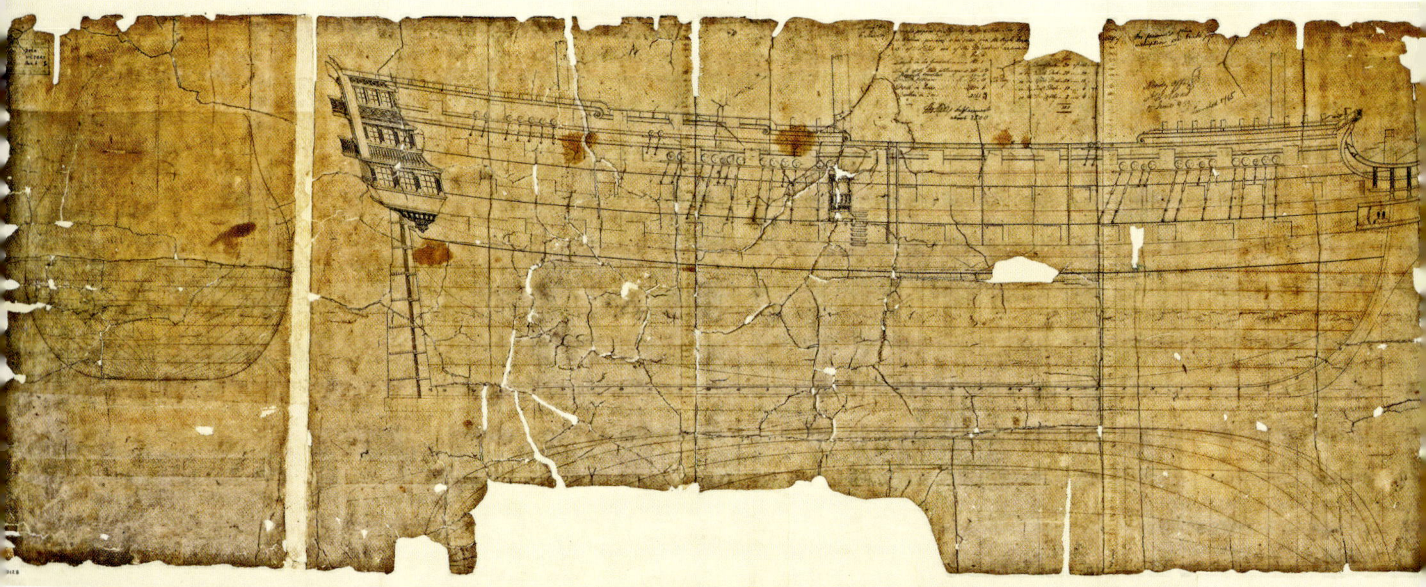

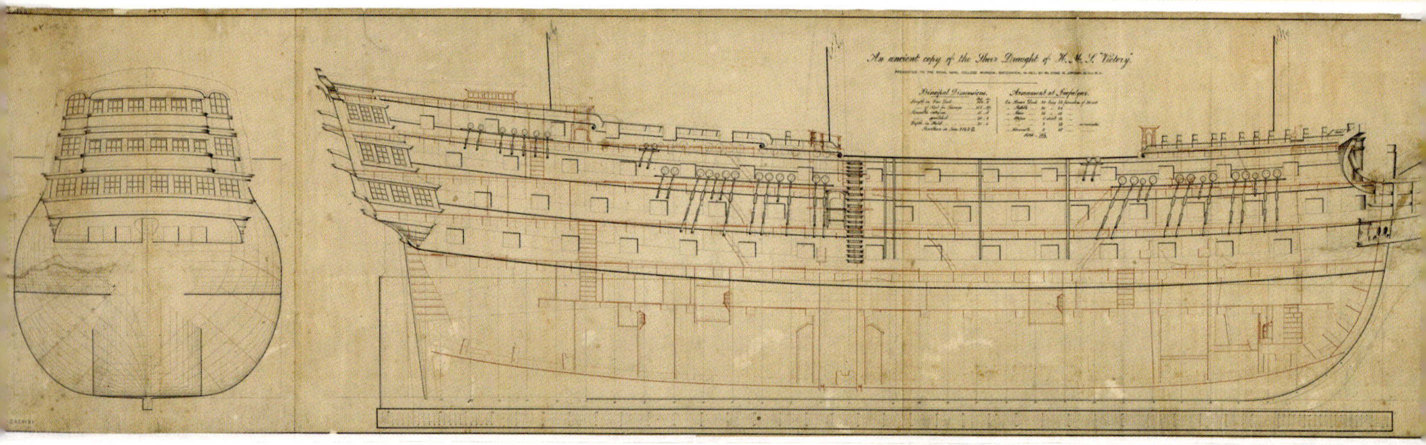

Upper: Now badly damaged, this is *Victory*'s original sheer draught representing Slade's design intentions. *(© National Maritime Museum, London J1849)*

Lower: Modern copy of *Victory*'s original sheer draught. It is not known when it was executed, although it lists the ship's armament at Trafalgar. It may date from the tenure of Sir Robert Seppings as Surveyor of the Navy (1813–1835) as it is known that he did much to preserve the historical achievements of his department. *(© National Maritime Museum, London J1850)*

lightest winds to bring her guns to bear. At the time *Victory* was designed and built, the principal design considerations were:

- *To make the Ship carry a good Sail.*
- *To make a Ship steer well, and Quickly Answer the helm.*
- *To make a Ship carry her Guns well out of the Water.*
- *To make a Ship go smoothly through the water without pitching hard,*
- *To make a Ship keep a good Wind.*
- *A large storage capacity allowing a Ship to operate independently from base for long periods,*
- *To withstand the onslaught of enemy shot in order to protect the Ship's own gun crews.*

[As summarised by Mungo Murray in his 1765 *Treatise on Ship-Building and Navigation: In Three Parts; Wherein the Theory, Practice, and Application of All the Necessary Instruments Are Perspicuously Handled*]

These requirements were vital because ships moved by the force of the wind, tide and current and the shape of the hull, placement of the masts, size and shape of the sails, and trim of the vessel were paramount to obtain the best sailing qualities. Naval encounters were an intricate ballet of manoeuvres – *tacking* (turning by bringing the head of the ship through the wind) and *wearing* (bringing the stern of the ship through the wind) and the sailing qualities of the ship played a significant role in how quickly and handily this could be accomplished. Forming a line of battle could take hours if not whole days, and the fleet that could form its battle line or column the fastest could gain the most advantageous position, such as the *weather gage* – the position of the ship to the windward of another that gives the initiative in manoeuvring.

Designers experimented with different full forms (called *lines*) and block models were built of new and proposed hulls to demonstrate their innovations to the Navy Board. At this time, ship design was much trial and error, experience, art, and inspiration. [Contrary to popular belief, the highly detailed official models that make up the collections held in maritime museums around the world today were not part of the design process – they often took as long to construct as the full-size ship and were primarily intended for display purposes.] The lines of captured enemy ships were always of intense interest to the naval powers of Europe. Their lines were taken off and copied, and captured ships that had particularly fine sailing qualities were taken into service and prized by their captains and crews alike. French frigates were of particular interest because they were known to handle well at sea, believed by many because their hull designs were supported by the burgeoning science of hydrodynamics that began in France in the 1730s. This research, for example, carried out systematic tests on the effect of shape on the rudder; where the centre of lateral resistance is best situated; the impact of buoyancy; and the location of the weight of the hull pushing downwards on stability on different hull forms. Much of this theory had little practical application, and the British relied more on experience and an empirical approach. Sir Thomas Slade (1703–1771), Surveyor of the Navy and previously Master Shipwright at the Royal Dockyards at Woolwich and Deptford, brought together experience and an instinctive understanding of the requirements in a career of outstanding warship design: but *Victory* is probably his masterpiece.

Commercial and imperial rivalries between Britain and France, and the antagonism between Prussia (then allied with Britain) and Austria (then allied with France and Russia) led to the outbreak of the Seven Years War (1756–1763) when Frederick the Great saw an opportunity to extend Prussian territory by invading Saxony. This action brought about simultaneous conflicts in Europe, North America, the West Indies, India and the Philippines – and Britain required ships for a global conflict. In December 1758 Parliament authorised a First Rate in addition to another eleven lesser rates. Slade's proposed First Rate specified:

- Length of the gun deck 186ft
- Length of the keel for tonnage 151ft 3⅝in
- Breadth moulded 50ft 6in
- Breadth extreme 51ft 10in
- To carry on the lower deck 30 guns of 42 pounds
- To carry on the middle deck 28 guns of 24 pounds
- To carry on the upper deck 30 guns of 12 pounds
- To carry on the after deck 10 guns of 6 pounds
- To carry on the forecastle 2 guns of 6 pounds

[Recorded in the Navy Board minutes of 6 June 1757. Cited in Goodwin, P, *HMS Victory, 1765–1812 (First rate ship of the line)*, Haynes, Sparkford 2012]

Construction of the new hull was ordered on 7 July1759 and commenced on the 23rd at Chatham Dockyard under Master Shipwright John Locke, and on 30 October 1760 the ship was named *Victory*. Locke passed away in 1762 and Edward Allin took the ship to completion.

Victory's construction followed the conventions and practices of the day with massive timbers of select species of wood hewn, shaped, and joined by hand. *Victory*'s timber had been sitting in store and seasoning (to diminish moisture content and dry out residual sap) since 1746. The stem post was made from three sections of compass (wood with natural curves) oak taken from trees at least 100 years of age. Each of her hull frames was constructed of a double layer of timbers with the joins between each layer staggered for strength. All of these elements were locked together with planking inside and out, and transverse deck beams supported by pillars and knees (brackets) for rigidity. The exterior planking up to the waterline was Baltic oak from East Prussia, and above that the hull was planked in English oak 4½in thick. All of these were fastened with iron bolts, some 12ft long, or oak or beech treenails that could be as large as 3ft long and 2in in diameter. The ship was made watertight by forcing *oakum* (tarred hemp or other natural fibres) into the seams and covering

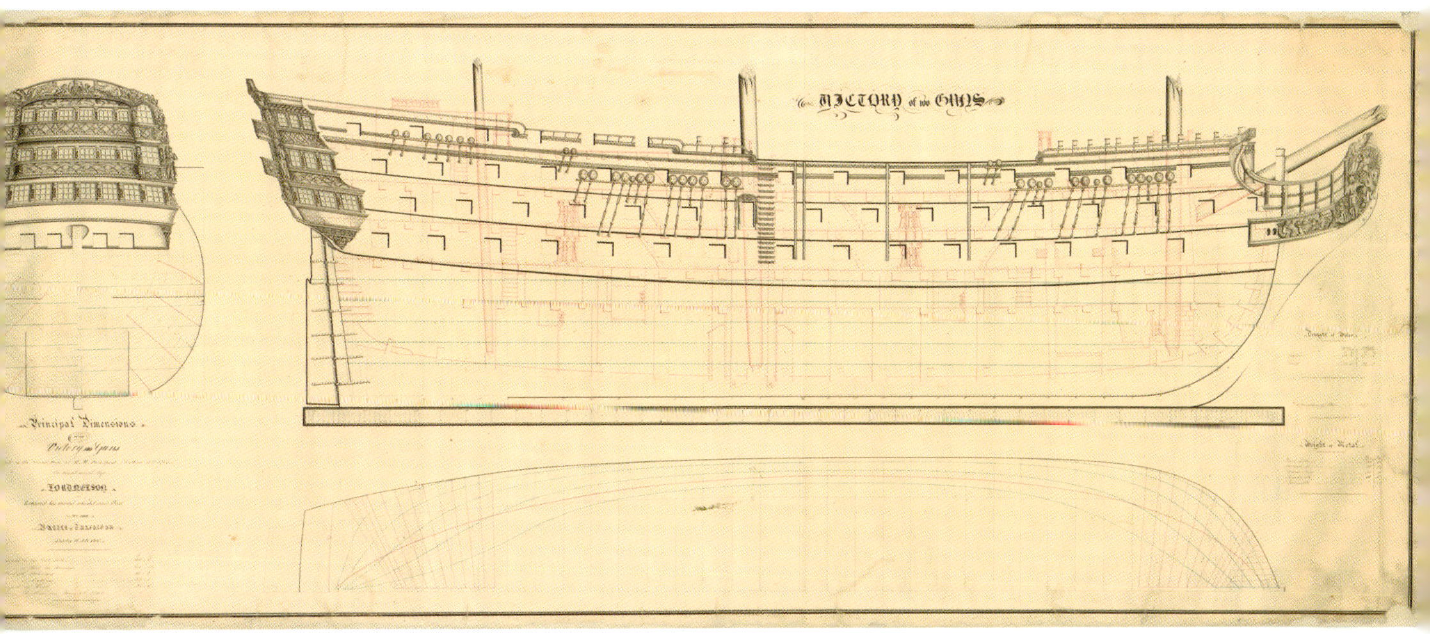

Reconstruction of *Victory*'s 'as fitted' draught. It is another undated, post-Trafalgar copy but is probably the most authoritative source for the ship's decorative scheme as completed. *(© National Maritime Museum, London J1842)*

A model of *Victory* in frame at the unusual scale of 1:180 [15ft to the inch]. Although the ship is shown on a conventional slipway, *Victory* was actually built in a drydock and floated out rather than launched. *(© National Maritime Museum, London F5834-001)*

it with hot pitch. The *Victory*'s hull required 2162 tons of timber, equivalent to 6000 oak trees from Kent, the New Forest (southwest Hampshire and southeast Wiltshire), and Germany.

The Seven Years War ended on 10 February 1763 with the signing of the Treaty of Paris, before *Victory* was finished. It was a resounding victory for Britain that stripped France of her North American and Indian colonies and gave birth to the British Empire. However, it left Britain with a massive debt, estimated at £122,603,336 on 5 January 1763 (over £22 billion in 2020), as well as huge new territories to administer. Not surprisingly, construction continued at a leisurely pace and it was not until 7 May 1765 that her hull was floated and ready for masting. *Victory* at completion measured 226ft 6in from figurehead to taffrail, had an estimated burden tonnage of 2162 tons, a calculated displacement of 3225 tons, and mean load draught of about 24ft. Despite her careful design and construction, as completed *Victory* had a pronounced list to port, and her gun ports were only 4ft 6in above the waterline – 9 inches lower than planned. A probable contributing factor was the different densities of timber (even if the same species) that add unexpected weight to the hull where it was used. Her cost including masts, yards, rigging and stores amounted to £63,176 3s 0d, or in today's money about £11,450,165.

Upon fitting out, she was immediately placed *in Ordinary* (reserve) – that is moored without stores, with upper masts and yards stowed ashore, and manned with just a carpenter, master gunner, and a small crew to work the pumps to deal with normal leakage. Sailing trials did not occur until four years later in 1769 but these extra years in Ordinary gave her timbers additional time to season and settle into their new configurations imparting greater strength and resiliency to the hull.

A three-decker ready for launch in a model of Chatham Dockyard dating from the 1770s. This gives a good impression of what *Victory*'s launch would have looked like, although the ship was actually built in one of the drydocks in the top left of the photograph. *(© National Maritime Museum, London B3110)*

Career Highlights

Victory's extensive active service career can be characterised as long periods of arduous blockade and convoy duty punctuated by a few great battles. Pitching seas and general wear and tear took more of a toll on the hull and rigging than the actions of the enemy. Timbers working loose, leakage, rot, and repairing all required *Victory* to spend a great deal of time in dock where the costs of repairs could exceed the cost of her original construction. Moreover, advances in ship design and the practical experience at sea led to the ship's rebuilding and alterations to get the best out of the hull. Otherwise, she sat at her moorings 'in Ordinary' for several years waiting for the next political crisis to have her readied for service once again.

VICTORY'S FIRST COMMISSION

The rebellion of the colonists in America, aided and abetted by the French brought *Victory* into her first commission as the flagship of Admiral Augustus Keppel in December 1776. He immediately ordered her 42-pounder guns replaced with 32-pounder guns, sacrificing some of the broadside weight of metal in favour of a faster rate of firing as the lighter guns were easier to handle in a seaway. In 1778 *Victory* saw her first significant action when a French fleet of 32 ships of the line, 7 frigates, 5 corvettes and a lugger, sailing from Brest under Amiral Louis Guillouet, Comte d'Orvilliers, was sighted off Cape Ushant on 23 July. Keppel's fleet had 30 ships of the line, 4 frigates and 2 fireships. For three days he tried to bring the French to action but d'Orvilliers, being under orders to avoid battle if possible in order to preserve the fleet, attempted to break out into the Atlantic. The two fleets manoeuvred until the morning of the 27th when the British got close enough to engage and Keppel ordered the fleet split into two squadrons with one under him and the one to rearward under Sir William Palliser.

The battle began at 11:20 and d'Orvilliers continued to tack and wear away, preventing the British from pressing home a concerted attack. When the fleets finally came into range, Keppel in *Victory* wanted to save his opening salvos for the French flagship *Bretagne* of 110 guns but his personal hubris resulted in *Victory* receiving six broadsides from several French ships without replying. This move badly damaged *Victory*'s rigging through the French practice of firing into the rigging to disable ships, rendering *Victory* difficult to manoeuvre. Only after he engaged *Bretagne* did Keppel move on to attacking the next six ships in the French line. The damage to *Victory's* rigging prevented her from getting into position to press the attack, and to make matters worse, Palliser's squadron was not formed in a line of battle but was instead a loose collection of ships that allowed the French to attack ships individually. Each one of Palliser's ships was savaged by the French one at a time because there was no disciplined line to offer mutually supported protection and attack. Despite having the advantage, the French did not press home the attacks but instead the fleet was seen to tack and sail south.

The reason for the French withdrawal remains unclear and d'Orvilliers accused the Duc de Chartres, Louis Phillipe II d'Orléans in *Saint Espirit* (80) and in command of the leading *Escadre Bleue* (Blue Squadron consisting of nine ships of the line) of not understanding or deliberately ignoring his order to press home the attack. For the British, Keppel signalled Palliser's ships to join him and form a line of battle to re-engage the French as they passed to leeward but Palliser could not or would not comply with the order, to which Keppel was forced to signal each individual ship. By the time each ship was in line, night had fallen and the next morning the French were 20 miles away so Keppel decided to return to Plymouth to have his ship repaired.

Chartres, on the other hand rushed to Paris with news of a great French victory that King Louis XVI was awakened from his bed to hear. Chartres became a fêted national hero and given a standing ovation at the opera, but that was short-lived when the details of his conduct during the battle became known to the point where he was ridiculed in the streets of Paris. It was no great French victory but an indecisive battle at best. As for Keppel, he was court-martialled but found not guilty of misconduct in action, but resigned anyway. Palliser was subject to an inconclusive inquiry on his conduct and the questions that followed dogged him for the rest of his career. As for *Victory*, she was given a refit in 1779 where her 42-pounder guns were restored, and in March 1780 her bottom was sheathed in copper.

Victory's next action occurred on 12 December 1781 under the flag of Rear Admiral Richard Kempenfelt that was known as the second battle of Cape Ushant. On 10 December a large French convoy loaded with reinforcements and stores for the French East and West Indies sailed from Brest escorted by 19 ships of the line under Luc Urbain de Bouexic, Comte de Guichen. A second convoy departed from Cádiz, Spain, with the 64-gun *Saint Michel* and the *Illustre* (74) escorting three transports headed for the Canary Islands to join up with Guichen. Kempenfelt was aware that the main convoy was sailing and engaged in a rigorous search for it with his squadron of 11 ships. He finally spotted Guichen on 12 December but discovered to his surprise that the escort had grown to 19 ships of the line. Kempenfelt decided his force of 11 ships was insufficient to attack and destroy them but in assessing the tactical situation, he noticed that Guichen's fleet was situated downwind of the convoy, and this allowed the British ships to sweep down and capture the transports before the French warships could intervene – he took 15 transport vessels whilst the large French escort could not double back in time. The French strategy to set sail during the December stormy season was a deliberate strategy in the hopes of bad weather hiding their movements and evading the British blockade. This strategy backfired as the remaining French transports and escorts alike were forced to return to port when a storm brewed up and they never made it to the Indies. The importance of the action really had little to do with the battle itself, but rather it triggered a series of official inquiries into the competence of the Royal Navy over its decision to send such a small force against the convoy. These inquiries and questions resulted in a Parliamentary vote of no-confidence and the fall of the Government of Lord Frederick North the next year that opened the way for a new government headed by Lord John Cavendish to negotiate the Treaty of Paris to end what was to become known as the American Revolution, and planted the seeds of a loyalist country in the future called Canada.

RELIEF OF GIBRALTAR

Victory herself also played shepherd to British convoys under the flag of Admiral Lord Howe to help end the siege of Gibraltar by joint French and Spanish forces. In April 1782 France and Spain signed the Treaty of Aranjuez in a collaborative effort to re-acquire territory lost to the British in the Seven Years War. The French and Spanish fleets were tasked with the blockade of Gibraltar at sea with a fleet of 49 ships of the line under the command of Almirante

The British fleet approaching Gibraltar on 11 October 1782 in a contemporary painting by Richard Paton. The centre ship is *Victory* flying Lord Howe's blue flag at the main. The Franco-Spanish fleet can be seen in the distance in Algeciras Bay. *(© National Maritime Museum, London BHC0453)*

Luis de Córdova y Córdova in the *Nuestra Señora de la Santísima Trinidad* (112). This ship was commonly known as the *Santísima Trinidad* and then the largest warship afloat. The British convoy sailed on 11 September escorted by 35 ships of the line destined for Gibraltar, with some intended to move on and to resupply the British colonies in the East and West Indies. Bad weather prevented the convoy from entering the Straits of Gibraltar until 11 October. Córdova was positioned to intercept in Algeciras Bay, but the British sailed right through the Straits towards the Moroccan coast in an attempt to shake off the Spanish. Córdova followed them through the Straits but lost them when the British took advantage of fair winds and turned around and re-entered the Straits, allowing the transports to reach Gibraltar safely between the 16th and 18th. The next day, Córdova's fleet was spotted east of Gibraltar and Howe weighed anchor and offered battle to Córdova by reducing sail to slow the British ships so they could come into contact with the Spanish. On the 20th Córdova held the weather gage, providing him with the option of accepting Howe's offer of battle or not on his terms. Córdova accepted battle at 13:00 and signalled his ships to engage in a general chase to bear down upon the British. The Spanish spent some time jostling to form their battle line while the British further reduced sail to tighten their fully formed line. At approximately 17:45 the leading ships (or *van*) of Córdova's fleet sailed down into range and opened fire.

The British returned fire but then Howe suddenly signalled 'retreat all sail' which turned his ships away from Córdova's battle line. This move put the British out of range from at least 14 French and Spanish ships in their line, and Howe quickly sailed away. Córdova attempted a general chase but Howe was following his orders to the letter to firstly deliver the convoy safely, and when this was accomplished, to return home directly. Despite following orders, Howe needed to explain why he did not take the opportunity to defeat the enemy and was reprimanded for not taking the initiative. From this time British commanders would take the opportunity to engage the enemy despite the odds for fear of removal from command and disgrace. Nevertheless, the success in resupplying the hard-pressed garrison at Gibraltar ensured its survival and strengthened the British position at peace talks.

From this action, it is interesting to note that the British ships showed a much greater ability to engage in or decline battle as the tactical situation evolved. This flexibility may be attributable to the fact that British three-deckers were handier than their opponents. The Spanish and French First Rates like the *Santísima Trinidad* (120) and *Purísima Concepción* (112), or the French 110-gun *Bretagne*, *Invincible*, *Majesteux* and *Royal Louis* in Córdova's fleet were all designed to be massive gun platforms but they lumbered at sea, slowing down and hampering the rest of their fleet in manoeuvres. Moreover, Córdova's fleet, most of which was Spanish (35 of 49 ships) were not as experienced in blockade duty, and were in poor condition having been battered by a storm the previous day on 10 October. The storm was so fierce that three ships were out of effective action by being blown ashore, out to sea, or under the guns of British forces in Gibraltar. More to the point, unlike the Spanish, the British ships were also copper-bottomed, allowing them greater speed and manoeuvrability.

THE FRENCH REVOLUTIONARY WARS

In 1789 the *Ancien Régime* of Bourbon France was beheaded to the cries of *Liberté, Égalité, et Fraternité* by the Paris mob. The French Republic was born and the monarchies of Europe joined together to prevent the spread of revolution and take advantage of the chaos in France. The fledgling French republic was not to be bullied and instead went on the offensive and conquered territories on the Italian peninsula, the Low Countries and the Rhineland with great revolutionary fervour. These wars brought *Victory* back into service under the flag of Samuel, Lord Hood. In January 1793, the British, supported by the Spanish fleet under Almirante Juan de Lángara, blockaded the French Mediterranean fleet based in Toulon. Shortly after Hood's arrival the Royalist citizens overthrew the Republican government of the city and invited the Anglo-Spanish fleet to occupy the port, but Royalist control was not assured. In the anchorage, three notable French ships, the *Pompée* (74), *Puissant* (74) and *Commerce de Marseille* (120) were crewed by French Royalists, but the fleet's sympathies, led by Contre-amiral Saint-Julien were decidedly Republican. As more and more republican troops, led by a young Captain Napoléon Bonaparte massed on the surrounding heights and the port and city eventually came under the Republican guns. The Anglo-Spanish fleet was forced to withdraw and Lángara ordered Don Pedro Cotiella, accompanied by Sir Sydney Smith, to take in boats to destroy the gunpowder stores held in hulks and in the arsenal. Smith's actions were fundamental in keeping the Republican forces in the harbour at bay while Captain Charles Hare brought in the fireship *Vulcan*; these actions succeeded in destroying six ships of the line and damaging five more. Beyond the loss of ships and powder, this action also destroyed the French fleet's timber store.

When Toulon was evacuated some 15 French ships of the line survived the attack and were repaired to later operate against the British at the Battle of Hyères in 1795 and the Nile in 1798. The French Royalist ships were taken into the Royal Navy. Despite the size of the *Commerce de Marseille*, she proved to be unstable in the Atlantic seas and spent the remainder of her career in port, as did *Puissant*. Only the *Pompée* saw active sea service under a British flag.

Victory received a repair in 1794 and returned to the Mediterranean in July 1795. Since 1793 the British blockade of French ports and the siege of Toulon had been very effective and the French navy was restricted to minor operations along the French coast. After the siege of Toulon the French worked to repair and rebuild their fleet and in March 1795 they were ready to take action once again. During a sortie by Vice-amiral Pierre Martin, the *Alceste* (32) and *Duquesne* (74) captured the British ship *Berwick* (74 guns, designed by Slade) which was caught sailing under jury rig owing to the loss of her masts during a strong gale. In French hands she was repaired at Toulon and taken into service. However, a mutiny broke out in parts of the newly rebuilt Toulon squadron in May. In a bid to re-establish control and instil revolutionary ideas in the mutinous ships, the National Convention in Paris ordered the sailors to set sail against the English and pledge to *'...laver leurs crimes dans le sang des ennemis de la République.'*['...wash their crimes in the blood of the enemies of the Republic', from Granier, H. (*Histoire des marins français (1789–1815)*, Marines éditions, Nantes 1998]

On 7 June, Martin set sail with 17 ships of the line and 6 frigates and was spotted by *Agamemnon* (64) who alerted Rear Admiral Hotham in *Victory* and his fleet then anchored in San Fiorenzo Bay, Corsica immediately set sail and gave chase. On the morning of the 13th Hotham found Martin just south of the Îsles d'Hyères. As the British ships came up, the French ships *Berwick* (74), *Tyrannacide* (74), *Aquilon* (74) and Martin's flagship *Alcide* (74) opened fire on the leading British ships *Culloden* (74), *Cumberland* (74) and *Victory* as they overtook them. *Alcide* damaged the rigging of *Culloden* and *Victory*, but the superior British gunnery soon damaged several French frigates and overwhelmed the *Alcide* who struck her colours at 14:00. The French frigates *Justice* (40) and *Alceste* (36) attempted to tow away their helpless flagship but the ship's boat carrying the tow rope was sunk by fire from *Victory*, and the French frigates sheered off under heavy fire. A fire broke out in *Alcide*'s maintop and a grenade ignited her magazines killing 300 seamen including her captain, Leblond Saint-Hylaire. Hotham ordered a withdrawal and the remainder of the French fleet was able to flee to Toulon. Hotham too was heavily criticised for failing to pursue and decisively destroy the French fleet. The consequences of his actions allowed a continued presence of French naval forces in the Mediterranean at a time when Britain could not well afford to keep ships there owing to a shortage of men and ships caused by growing commitments in the Atlantic. The British eventually withdrew their fleet from the Mediterranean temporarily allowing it to become what was termed a 'French lake'.

Battle of Cape St Vincent, painting by Robert Cleveley. The *Victory* is shown raking a Spanish three-decker, identified by the artist as *Salvador del Mundo* but the incident depicted probably involved the *Principe de Asturias*. (© National Maritime Museum, London BHC0485)

BATTLE OF CAPE ST VINCENT

On 3 December 1795 Admiral Sir John Jervis hoisted his flag in *Victory* and took over the blockade of Toulon. On land the French had won several decisive victories against Britain's ally Austria and in October 1796 Spain changed sides and allied themselves to Republican France. The combined Spanish and French fleet in the Mediterranean now numbered 38 ships of the line that greatly outnumbered the British Mediterranean Fleet of 15 ships forcing the British, as noted earlier, to evacuate their positions in Corsica and Elba to Gibraltar. Jervis's fleet withdrew to the Tagus in Portugal.

On 1 February 1797 a Spanish fleet of 27 ships under Don José de Córdoba left Cartagena intending to join up with a French fleet sailing from Brest to escort a large merchant convoy to Cádiz. However, a strong easterly wind blew Córdoba's fleet farther into the Atlantic than intended. As the Spanish started to work their way towards Cádiz they were spotted on 11 February by Commodore Horatio Nelson onboard the frigate *Minerve* (36). Thanks to heavy fog *Minerve* passed through the Spanish fleet undetected and Nelson was able to alert Jervis of their position. Unaware of the British presence, Córdoba continued toward Cádiz where on the 14th Jervis learnt that the Spanish fleet was just 35 miles away and began to organise his fleet for battle.

In the early morning, Jervis saw that the Spanish were also formed into two loose columns. The first to windward (upwind from the direction of the wind) composed of 18 ships to the north, and 9 ships in their leeward column (downwind of the direction of the wind) to the south. His battle plan was to form his ships into two columns as well, a windward column of eight ships followed by a second column to leeward of six ships. The plan was to have the British columns sail in between the Spanish columns allowing each British ship to fire in both directions while the Spanish fire was limited for fear of hitting one of their own ships on the other side.

This plan changed around 10:30 when the Spanish weather column was seen to wear suggesting that they might form a line to put the smaller British column under fire from the larger Spanish division. In response, Jervis gave his order: 'Form in a line of battle ahead and astern of *Victory* as most convenient' to transform the two British columns into a single line. At 11:12 Jervis made his next signal: 'Engage the enemy' and then at 11:30: 'Admiral intends to pass through enemy line' meaning the British line would sail south between the two Spanish columns. Because the Spanish columns were not parallel to each other, but the windward one to the north and the leeward south, Jervis signalled at 13:05 for each ship to 'Take suitable stations for mutual support and engage the enemy as coming up in succession'. This signal instructed the ships to pass in between the Spanish columns and engage both of them as they came into range. After each ship engaged and passed the Spanish leeward column, each ship was to tack and sail north to come up and engage Córdoba's weather column a second time. This caused the British line to begin to take on the shape of the letter J as each ship tacked and headed north.

Córdoba realising the British line now lay between him and his leeward division in the south, ordered his lee division to put about on the port tack with the intention of breaking the British line at the point where the British ships were tacking in succession. The Spanish ships bore down on this point and opened fire causing damage to *Orion* (74) and *Colossus* (74) as they came to the tacking point. As the *Victory* came to the tacking point, her speed in closing the gap between herself and the *Principe de Asturias* (112) carrying Vice-Admiral Joaquin Moreno caused the Spanish ship to tack too late to bring her broadside to bear against *Victory*. Instead Moreno received two devastating raking broadsides from *Victory*'s guns.

The British line had now become a long U shape with the ships at the head and at the end of the line in the same proximity to the Spanish weather column. Nelson (now moved into *Captain*, 74) realised that if Jervis' order was followed to the letter half of the British fleet would be effectively out of the battle and too far away from the Spanish weather column to catch them. There were enough British ships moving southward following Jervis' order towards the tacking point to engage the Spanish lee column so he ordered his ship out of the battle line and passed to the head of the British line crossing the bows of five large Spanish vessels. *Captain* was followed out of the line by *Diadem* (64) and *Excellent* (74) and engaged the *Santísima Trinidad* (with armament now increased to 130 guns), the *San Josef* (112), the *Salvador del Mundo* (112) and the *San Nicolas* (80). The *Captain* was badly damaged by these Spanish behemoths, so Nelson laid *Captain* along the starboard quarter of the *San Nicolas* and boarded. When she surrendered, more men were ordered aboard the *San Nicolas* and charged on to take the *San Josef* using the *San Nicolas* as a bridge. At 16:15 the fighting was all but over and 15 British ships had defeated a Spanish fleet of 27, with four of them captured, including two First Rates.

Jervis signalled his fleet to cover the prizes and disabled vessels, and the frigates directed to take the prizes in tow. At 16:39 the fleet was ordered to take station in line astern of *Victory* with *Britannia* (100) and *Orion* firing on the departing *Santísima Trinidad* who had struck her colours but managed to escape with the help of *Infante*

Victory off Belem Castle in the Tagus while the flagship of Sir John Jervis in 1797. Watercolour by Thomas Buttersworth, who was serving in the fleet at the time, so may be regarded as a view from life. Note the ship's paint scheme. *(© National Maritime Museum, London PW5945)*

Don Pelayo (74) and *San Pablo* (74). This loss of the Spanish ships fundamentally changed the balance of sea power in the Mediterranean that allowed Jervis to easily blockade Spanish and French ports until the British were able to reinforce and return to the Mediterranean with a squadron under Nelson who finally wrested control for Britain at the Battle of the Nile in August 1798. For Cordóba, he was dismissed from the Armada and further humiliated by being forbidden to ever appear again at the Spanish court.

Victory's service career immediately after the Battle of Cape St Vincent was much less eventful. In September she served as a troop transport, and was finally ordered to Chatham where a survey showed that her timbers had worked loose and she was paid off at the close of 1797. She was refitted as a hospital ship and moored in the River Medway, and a conversion to a prison hulk ordered. This order was changed to a 'Great Repair' – the most substantial category of reconstruction – probably due to the fact that repairing *Victory* was quicker and much more economical than building a new First Rate. The Great Repair was completed in April 1803 and *Victory*'s appearance was transformed to largely what we see today. She emerged much more modern-looking, her old-fashioned open stern closed in and forecastle, quarterdeck, and poop bulwarks ordered heightened to form solid barricades that afforded better protection to the gun crews and men on these decks.

BATTLE OF TRAFALGAR

The failure of the Treaty of Amiens (1802) ended the short-lived peace between France and Britain because neither side trusted the other and each accused their opponent of not fulfilling the terms of the agreement. War was declared again on 18 May 1803 and *Victory* sailed for the Mediterranean as the flagship of the now Lord Nelson on the 20 May. For two years she commanded the blockade of the French base at Toulon. On 18 May 1804 Napoléon Bonaparte crowned himself Emperor and Imperial France, now at the height of her power was born to the cries of *Vive la France! Vive l'Empereur!* Having abandoned the massive but impractical scheme to invade England, La Grande Armée marched across Europe to *La Victoire est à Nous!* Following an epic chase to the Caribbean and back in pursuit of a French fleet, on 15 August 1805 *Victory* was ordered home to Portsmouth and underwent minor repairs that added two 68-pounder carronades to her forecastle making her into a 104-gun First Rate. On 28 September, *Victory* with Lord Nelson rejoined the fleet off Cádiz. A month later, on 21 October, the Battle of Trafalgar was fought.

Napoléon had been determined to invade Britain, but a successful landing hinged on being able to control the Channel by destroying the Royal Navy to allow La Grande Armée safe passage. Having failed to successfully execute Napoleon's elaborate plan to decoy the British fleet away, Amiral Pierre-Charles Villeneuve on his flagship *Bucentaure* (80) decided to sail from Cádiz on 18 October with overall command of the Combined Fleet of 18 French and 15 Spanish ships under the command of Almirante Federico Carlos Gravina y Nápoli. This fleet included the massive *Santísima Trinidad* (up gunned again to 136 guns), the *Principe de Asturias* (112), and the *Santa Ana* (112). Nelson had at his command 27 ships formed into two columns, the windward column led by himself in *Victory*, and the lee column led by Vice-Admiral Cuthbert Collingwood in *Royal Sovereign* (100). Nelson's plan was to split the Combined Fleet's line in two places effectively reducing Villeneuve's fleet by one third as the French van would have to take time to turn back and tack against the wind into the battle, whilst the other two-thirds would be locked into a general mêlée against superior British gunnery. Interestingly, Villeneuve anticipated Nelson's tactics and instead of organising his fleet to take advantage of the sailing and fighting qualities of each ship, he gave orders that would place a Spanish ship between two French ones in the battle line. This was borne out of the uneasy alliance between Imperial France and Spain, and the distrust of the Spanish who it was thought might just sail away.

It is in this battle that *Victory* and Nelson became synonymous. There are many scholarly and first-hand accounts of the action by noted historians that describe each minute of the battle between each ship of these fleets. *Victory's* role was central and although she reached the French and Spanish lines after *Royal Sovereign*, she quickly became the focus of the fight. *Victory* led the Windward Squadron towards a point in between *Redoutable* (74) commanded by the fiery Captaine Jean Jacques Étienne Lucas, who was deter-

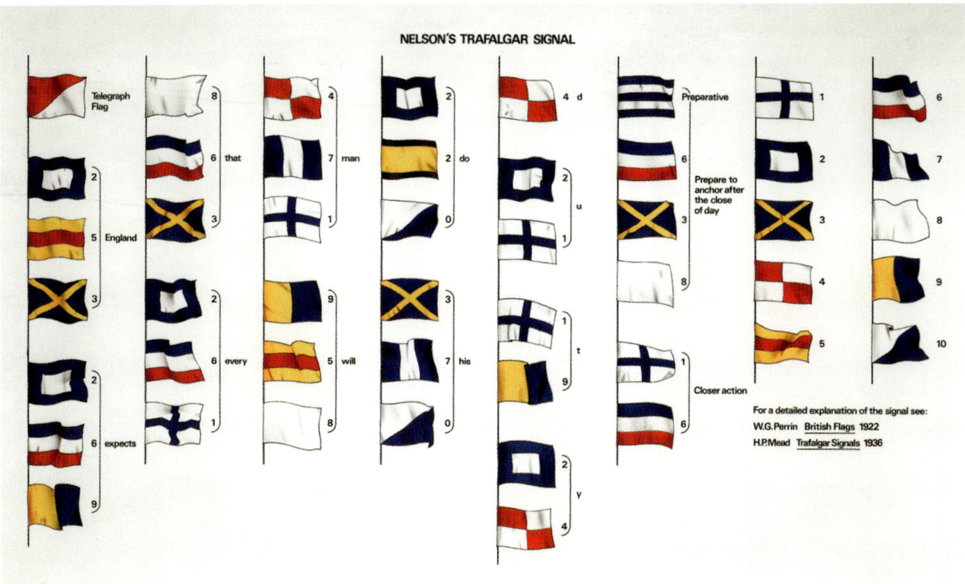

Left: Nelson's famous 'England expects...' signal in Popham's code. Modern research suggests his original intention was to begin the signal 'Nelson confides [*ie* has confidence] that ...', a more personal and less hectoring sentiment, but his flag lieutenant proposed changes to use fewer flags, and so a legendary signal was born. *(© National Maritime Museum, London D8080)*

mined to take a British ship and trained his crew in boarding tactics, and the French flagship *Bucentaure*. The Combined Fleet at this point in the line was crowded and a little confused caused by the French and Spanish ships attempting to get into the precise order dictated by Villeneuve. There seemed to be no way through so *Victory* simply rammed the *Redoutable*, firing one broadside into her and the other into the *Bucentaure* and the Spanish flagship *Santísima Trinidad*. The British ship *Téméraire* (98) came up and flanked *Redoutable* on the far side, firing all her broadsides at point blank range as *Victory* locked yards with the *Redoutable* and each fired into each other only feet apart. The *Redoutable*'s crew included an infantry corps who gathered with seamen for an attempt to board and seize *Victory*. *Victory*'s gunners mustered on deck to repel and her guns ceased firing while the gunners were forced back below decks by grenades hurled onto her decks from the soldiers in the *Redoutable's* rigging. With the French preparing to board *Victory*, *Temeraire* approached from the starboard bow of *Redoutable* and fired on the men gathering on the decks with a carronade ending the boarding attempt. At 13:55, Lucas in *Redoutable*, with 99 fit men (out of 643) and severely wounded himself,

Below: A bird's-eye panorama of the Battle of Trafalgar, painted by Nicholas Pocock, one of the most meticulous of all marine painters. The opening phase of the battle is shown, with the Combined Fleet disposed from top left to bottom right; the two British columns approach from the right, with Nelson's Windward division nearer and Collingwood's Lee line further off, both flagships being already engaged. *(© National Maritime Museum, London BHC0548)*

Above: *Victory* under tow to Gibraltar after the Battle of Trafalgar. Painting by Clarkson Stansfield. *(© National Maritime Museum, London D2575)*

Opposite, top: *Victory* in 1807 showing her appearance after the Trafalgar repair. Print by Robert Dodd. *(© National Maritime Museum, London PY0724)*

Opposite, bottom: *Victory* in the 1860s. Watercolour by Mackenzie Thompson. *(© National Maritime Museum, London PW7815)*

surrendered. Nelson was dead, the sniper's shot probably dividing the left pulmonary artery and damaging the spinal cord later in its course. [Wang, D, El-Masry, W S, Crumplin, M, Eisenstein, S, Pusey, R J, & Meagher, T, 'Admiral Lord Nelson's death: known and unknown – A historical review of the anatomy' in *Spinal Cord*, 43, (2005), pages 573–576]

As the British columns entered the battle the centre of the Combined Fleet was overwhelmed, losing 22 vessels. Among the captured French ships were *L'Aigle* (74), *Algésiras* (74), *Berwick* (74), *Bucentaure* (74), *Fougueux* (74) *Intrépide* (74), *Redoutable*, and *Swiftsure* (74). The Spanish ships taken were *Argonauta* (80), *Bahama* (74), *Monarca* (74), *Neptuno* (74), *San Agustín* (74), *San Ildefonso* (74), *San Juan Nepomuceno* (74), *Santísima Trinidad*, and *Santa Ana*. Of these, *Redoutable* sank, and *Santísima Trinidad* and *Argonauta* were later scuttled by the British. *Achille* exploded, *Intrépide* and *San Augustín* burned, and *L'Aigle*, *Berwick*, *Fougueux*, and *Monarca* were wrecked in a gale following the battle. The cut-off van under Contre-amiral Dumanoir Le Pelley in *Formidable* (80) attempted to turn and make a furtive return to the battle but instead led his ships away and made for Toulon, thinking it wiser saving his ships to help escort La Grande Armée across the Channel. Ironically, Napoléon had already abandoned his plans for the invasion of Britain before Trafalgar was fought, deciding instead to take on the combined armies of Russia and Austria at Austerlitz in what is known as the 'Battle of the Three Emperors'.

Victory's damage at Trafalgar was so extensive she took on 12 inches of water per hour despite pumping tons from the hull. She was towed to Gibraltar for temporary repairs, and from there to Chatham for full repairs on 6 March 1806. There she was re-coppered, fitted with new masts and spars, re-rigged and on the quarterdeck her guns were replaced with eight 32-pounder carronades. She remained at her moorings until March 1807 and on 11 November was re-rated as a Second Rate of 98 guns and her masts and spars reduced accordingly. Her lower deck armament was further reduced by two 32-pounders, and on the middle deck all her 24-pounders were replaced by 18-pounders, reducing the stress on her timbers.

THE TRAFALGAR ANTICLIMAX AND RESTORATION

In March 1808 she was recommissioned as the flagship of Rear Admiral Richard Saumarez and was deployed to the Baltic. Tsar Alexander I and Napoléon signed the

Victory undergoing her original restoration. Watercolour by William Lionel Wyllie. *(© National Maritime Museum, London PW1490)*

Treaty of Tilsit that allied the two empires for a short time after the Russians were defeated at the Battle of Friedland. The treaty brought the Russians into Napoléon's 'Continental System' that blocked any trade with Britain. The vast Russian navy was now a potential threat and Saumarez attempted to draw the Baltic fleet into battle. The Russians never accepted the challenge because Tsar Alexander never really intended to live up to the terms of the agreement and trade continued. Napoléon knew that he could not trust his allies, and about this time, other agreements and alliances began to fray. In particular the alliance between Spain and France ended when Napoléon decided to occupy Spain on the pretext they

Victory repainted in the 'terracotta' scheme in November 2016, representing the latest research into the ship's Trafalgar appearance. *(Author's collection)*

were marching through Spain to take Portugal, who was Britain's oldest ally. It was a *de facto* invasion and occupation of her ally and the Spanish rose in rebellion. British troops went to Spain to support the uprising, but were initially beaten back by the French. *Victory* assisted with the evacuation of the retreating British army gathering in Corunna in January 1809, and later *Victory* returned to the peninsula ferrying British and Portuguese troops under the command of the Sir Arthur Wellesley that finally ousted the French from Spain at the Battle of Vitoria in 1813.

On 7 November 1812 *Victory* arrived at Spithead, paid off and was placed in Ordinary. A Great Repair commenced in 1814 and when completed in 1816, she emerged from Portsmouth as a newly updated ship incorporating the reforms of Sir Robert Seppings. Most notable was the new built-up 'round bow' and beakhead. In 1817 she was re-rated as a First Rate but sat at her moorings until 21 January 1825 when she became the flagship of the Port Admiral or the Captain of the Ordinary (the officer in charge of all ships at Portsmouth placed in Ordinary). In 1847 she was made the stationary flagship of the Commander-in-Chief. A decade later she required significant repair and it was decided she should be permanently moored in the harbour. She resumed her role as stationary flagship until 1869 when she was paid off and served as a storage tender. She was docked in 1887 due to a severe leak and her wooden lower masts were replaced by hollow wrought iron masts to further reduce weight and stress on the old hull. She remained in this state until 1903.

On 23 October 1903 *Victory* was damaged below the portside waterline when the tugs towing the ironclad turret ship *Neptune* to the breakers lost control in rough weather. She was repaired and sat deteriorating at her moorings until 1920 when the Society for Nautical Research championed and led the restoration of the ship. On 16 December 1921 she was moved to Portsmouth's Basin Number 2. The decision was made to restore her as close as possible to her Trafalgar appearance. Opened to the public in 1928, she has been visited by millions of visitors since. Her restoration is on on-going concern because her timbers are under constant threat from death-watch beetles, wet and dry rot, and even the Luftwaffe when she was struck by a bomb in 1941. Archaeological and historical work continues, which now has her fully repainted into a new 'terracotta' scheme thought to be worn at Trafalgar as opposed to the familiar dark yellow ochre stripes she had sported since her restoration.

SERVICE HISTORY

Date	Event
23 July 1759	Keel laid. Old single dock, Number 2 Dock, Chatham Royal Dockyard.
30 October 1760	Named *Victory*.
7 May 1765	Hull launched; placed in Ordinary in the Medway.
1769	Sailing trials.
1769–1771	Returned to moorings; placed in Ordinary at Upnor.
1771	Ordered to be prepared for war and hull planking found to be eaten by worm. Given a 'Middling Repair' costing £4276 (now about £738,024).
1775	Worm damage repaired costing £3075 (now £507,990).
1776	Brought out of Ordinary and outfitted as flagship of the Channel Fleet for Admiral Hon. Augustus Keppel. 42-pounder guns replaced with 32-pounders. Cost of fitting out was £13,962 (£2,274,036).
March 1778	Great Britain declares War on France. *Victory* at sea.
7 July 1778	Indecisive action off Cape Ushant.
March 1779	Keppel strikes flag, and flag of Admiral Sir Charles Hardy is raised. *Victory* receives refit. 42-pounder guns reshipped and remained until 1798. Refit cost £8301 (£1,476,811).
October 1779	Hardy dies and succeeded by Admiral Sir Frances Geary.
April 1780	Geary resigns due to ill health and was succeeded by Vice Admiral George Darby.
March 1780	Darby transfers his flag to *Britannia*. *Victory* becomes a 'private ship' (a ship commanded by a captain which is not a flagship) until hauled out for a refit. Copper plating fitted to underwater hull. Cost of refit £8941 (£1,641,170). *Victory* becomes the flagship of Vice Admiral William Drake.
July–August 1781	Flagship of Vice Admiral Hyde Parker.
September 1781–March 1782	Flagship of Rear Admiral Richard Kempenfelt.
20 April 1782	Admiral Lord Howe hoists flag. Present at relief of Gibraltar, action off Cape Spartel in October where she suffered damage to foreyard, hull, and sails.
14 November 1782–1789	Howe strikes flag, the ship paid off, and receives major refit at cost of £15,373 (£2,653,333). Returned to reserve and moored in Portsmouth harbour for five years. In 1787 prepared for war, but an assessment found her to require considerable repair. Forecastle lengthened and masts moved to compensate. Returned to reserve.
August 1790	Relations with Spain worsened and *Victory* fitted for sea at cost of £6451 (£1,008,099). Put to sea under flag of Lord Howe.

Continued overleaf:

February 1791	Returned for refit for essential repairs costing £3376 (£520,534).
December 1792–early 1795	Selected flagship for Mediterranean fleet and fitted for sea. Cost £8177 (£1,244,195). Part of the Toulon blockade. Returned to Portsmouth in December 1794 for refit and a flying jib-boom added to increase sail area and improve manoeuvrability.
13 July 1795	Action off Hyères.
3 December 1795–14 February 1797	Admiral Sir John Jervis hoists flag and Battle of Cape St Vincent.
November 1797	*Victory* paid off at Chatham and relegated to her moorings as a hospital ship for prisoners of war.
1798	Admiralty considered reducing her to a prison hulk, but senior officers intervened given her historical status and she continued to serve as a hospital ship.
Early 1800–11April 1803	Docked for Middling Repair, but extensive defects found given a Great Repair taking three years. Stern galleries closed in and bulwarks raised. Cost £70,933 (£7,456,992). Vice-Admiral Viscount Lord Nelson hoists flag.
20 May 1803	*Victory* sails for the Mediterranean to begin the 18-month blockade of Toulon.
18 August 1805	Returned to Portsmouth after 27 months at sea including a chase of the French fleet to the West Indies. Short refit and two 68-pounder carronades and two 12-pounders installed on forecastle bringing armament to 104 guns.
14 September 1805	Nelson rejoins *Victory*.
21 October 1805	Battle of Trafalgar.
28 October 1805	Extensively damaged, *Victory* reaches Gibraltar and anchors in Rosia Bay. Temporary repairs.
4 November 1805	*Victory* sails for home and puts into Plymouth for additional temporary repairs.
11 December 1805	Arrives in Medway and Nelson's body landed.
15 January 1806	Paid off for survey.
6 March 1806	*Victory* entered Number 2 Dock at Chatham to repair battle damage and rearmed. Returned to moorings. Total cost £9936 (£911,904).
March 1807	Leak discovered and docked for underwater check and extensive dry rot discovered.
11 November 1807	Downgraded to a Second Rate of 98 guns.
April 1808	Sailed for Gothenburg under the flag of Vice-Admiral Sir James de Saumarez, new commander of Baltic fleet.
10 November 1808	Returned to Portsmouth for essential repairs.
10 December 1808	Under command of Captain J C Searle assisted in the evacuation of Sir John Moore's army from Corunna.
23 January 1809	Returned to Plymouth.
3 February 1810	Returned to Baltic under Saumarez.
4 December 1810	Returned to England and converted to troop carrying under Rear-Admiral Sir Joseph Yorke.
26 March 1811	Returned to Portsmouth.
2 May 1811	Sailed under Saumerez for another tour of Baltic duty.
25 December 1811	Returned to Portsmouth and refit.
17 April 1812	Sailed for a fifth Baltic deployment.
7 November 1812	Anchored at Spithead.
30 November 1812	Paid off at Portsmouth. End of 47 years of seagoing service.
1813	At moorings.
March 1814	Great Repair. Docked and many defects found, and given a major rebuilding incorporating Seppings's reforms such as round bow completed early 1816. Cost £79,772 (£7,952,443).
1817	Reclassified as a First Rate.
1823	Refit for guard ship duties. Cost £17, 010 (£2,070,564).
24 January 1824	Made Port Admiral's flagship.
1830	Surveyed and paid off, and placed in Ordinary. Headquarters ship of the reserve fleet and residence of the Captain of the Ordinary.
5 October 1831	Upgraded and commissioned as flagship of the Port Admiral.
1840	Moved to moorings off Gosport.
1869	Paid off as flagship.
1869–1891	Served as tender to *Duke of Wellington*, the new flagship of the Port Admiral. Emergency docking in 1887 to repair a serious leak.
1891 to present	Reinstated as flagship of the C-in-C Portsmouth.
1903	Rammed at her moorings by *Neptune*.
15 June 1921	Lord Milford Haven of the Society for Nautical Research submits a paper that *Victory* is decaying.
14 January 1922	*Victory* docked in Number 2 Dock at Portsmouth as a permanent home. Fundraising begins for restoration to 'near Trafalgar appearance'.
17 July 1928	Fully restored ship unveiled and inspected by HM George V and open to the public.
10 March 1941	Damaged by a Luftwaffe bomb; repaired back to restored condition.
2015–2016	Repainted in her 'terracotta and dark grey' scheme dated to 1805 through archaeological research.

Note: Value of repairs in 2020 in brackets. Computed using Bank of England inflation calculator.

Model Products

The Modelmaker's Challenge

There have been kits of *Victory* in styrene, white metal, wood, card, resin and 3D printed models, ensuring there is one available to suit your budget and preferences. The modelmaker's challenge will be to recreate the masts, yards, rigging and sails authentically. In particular installing the correct rigging lines and keeping them in scale. Highly recommended is *Rigging Period Ship Models* by Lennarth Petersson. Step by step instructions show you how every line is rigged on a frigate, and easily adaptable to a First Rate. Rigging also extends to the guns, lifelines, hammock nettings, anchor cables, and everything is tied (seized) in place with rope and line. Rigging is especially a challenge on models smaller than 1:100 and require miniaturist techniques. Phillip Reed's *Modelling Sailing Men of War* and *Period Ship Modelmaking* books not only cover miniature rigging, but sail making, hull coppering and a host of techniques useful in refining plastic kit parts or scratch building better ones. Models larger than 1:100 scale can be rigged just like the real ship using blocks, deadeyes, thimbles and all the gear found on *Victory*. Reference to the extensive drawings and photos found in John McKay's *Victory* and Allan McGowan's *HMS Victory: Her Construction, Career, and Restoration* will reveal the run of every line, how the sails were constructed, as well as details of the hull and deck planking, every fitting, and ship's boats in detail.

Victory is often modelled in 'harbour rig' where no sails are *bent* (secured to a yard), or in several different sail configurations ranging from full sail to furled sails and in between. *Victory* was bound by and propelled by the forces of nature and capturing this fundamental aspect is essential for an authentic model. Sails, flags and pennants must also be shaped to flutter in the wind and some rigging lines will need a windblown catenary worked into them. Finally, ensure that your *Victory* is flying the correct ensigns, pennants and signals. Coming to understand how Sir Home Popham's naval code was used and exactly where the flags were hoisted ensures that Nelson's last signals, '*England expects...*' followed by '*Engage the Enemy More Closely*' is read by all.

SAILS OF A 100-GUN SHIP:
1. Spritsail 2. Spritsail Topsail 3. Fore Course (Or Fore Sail)
4. Fore Topsail 5. Fore Topgallant Sail 6. Fore Royal Sail
7. Fore Staysail 8. Fore Topgallant Staysail 9. Jib
10. Flying Jib 11. Main Course (Or Main Sail) 12. Main Topsail
13. Main Topgallant Sail 14. Main Royal Sail 15. Main Staysail
16. Main Topmast Staysail 17. Middle Staysail 18. Main Topgallant Staysail
19. Mizzen Tosail 20. Mizzen Topgallant Sail 21. Spanker
22. Mizzen Staysail 23. Mizzen Topmast Staysail 24. Mizzen Topgallant Staysail

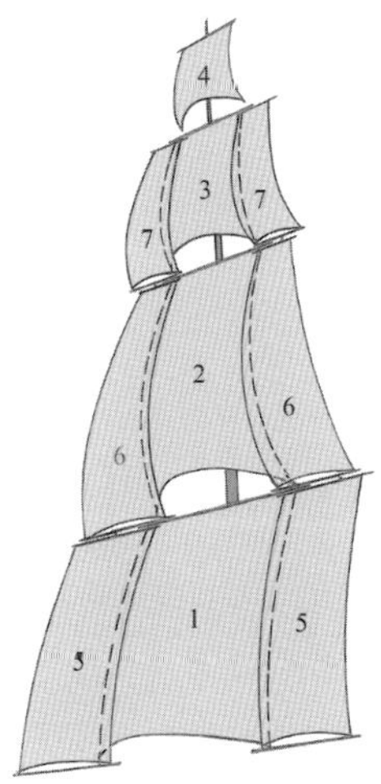

MAIN MAST STUDDING SAILS
(Fore Mast is Similar)
1. Main Course 2. Main Topsail
3. Main Topgallant Sail 4. Main Royal Sail
5. Main Lower Studding Sail
6. Main Topmast Studding sail
7. Main Topgallant Studding Sail

LANGTON MINIATURES *VICTORY* 1:1200 Scale

Langton Miniature's *Victory* is cast in white metal with all of her gun ports open. The hull casting is deeper below the waterline allowing it to be set into a plaster seascape as opposed to sitting unrealistically on top of it. The hull details are quite distinct and helps guide your paintbrush, and allows for highlights and shadows to be more easily painted. The transom is a separate piece with windows, decoration, and lanterns distinctly moulded in place. The deck planking is represented by unrealistically spaced recessed lines, but they are quite shallow and after a coat of primer will reduce their prominence to satisfy the scale enthusiast. The upper gun deck is represented by a shallow recess with boat beams moulded in place. No ship's boats are included for the beams or for the quarter davits. These small boats are easily carved from square piece of basswood if desired. The hull bulwarks are all detailed with nettings filled with hammocks.

Masts and yards are a single casting and sails supplied in either white metal or etched from thin brass sheet. In this tiny scale, the mast and sails are over-scale as befits a wargame miniature that is pushed across a tabletop seascape. However, the different sections of the masts and yards are cast in the correct proportions to one another and look correct. If that does not satisfy, new masts and yards can be made from brass rod or wood dowel with sails from paper using the kit parts as a guide. Optional generic etched brass ratlines are offered that look good on the gaming table with some representative stays from thread, wire, or elastic thread.

Langton also offers seascape bases in resin or white metal, and proper flags, pennants, and signal flags in the correct pattern for the different years in service (pre- and post-1801) and different admirals (White, Blue, and Red Ensigns) as required.

GHQ 100-GUN SHIP (CAN BE USED AS *VICTORY*)

1:1200 Scale

Cast in pewter, the hull details are extremely fine and remarkably in scale – including miniscule stern lanterns. The waist is a deeply cast recess to give a most convincing impression of the lower deck with boat beams in place. The separate stern gallery is highly detailed and the decks are cast smooth. The gun ports are closed. The kit also includes perfectly cast anchors and ship's boats. Hammock netting only appears in the ship's waist, and the forecastle, quarterdeck, and poop bulwarks are not heightened and inaccurate for Trafalgar.

The masts, yards, and sails and cast as a single unit in either of two configurations described as 'full sail' and 'battle sail'. Full sail includes all the primary courses (no studdingsails) unfurled and billowing in the wind, whereas battle sail has the main and fore courses loosely furled. GHQ moulds a lug between the front face of the mast and back of each sail for strength. Generic assembly instructions suggest adding just a few lines of standing and running rigging to give a realistic impression. Painting instructions are generic so do not follow them for *Victory*. All in all, this is a fine miniature and with some simple scratch building can be made into an excellent replica for the gaming table or a dramatic diorama.

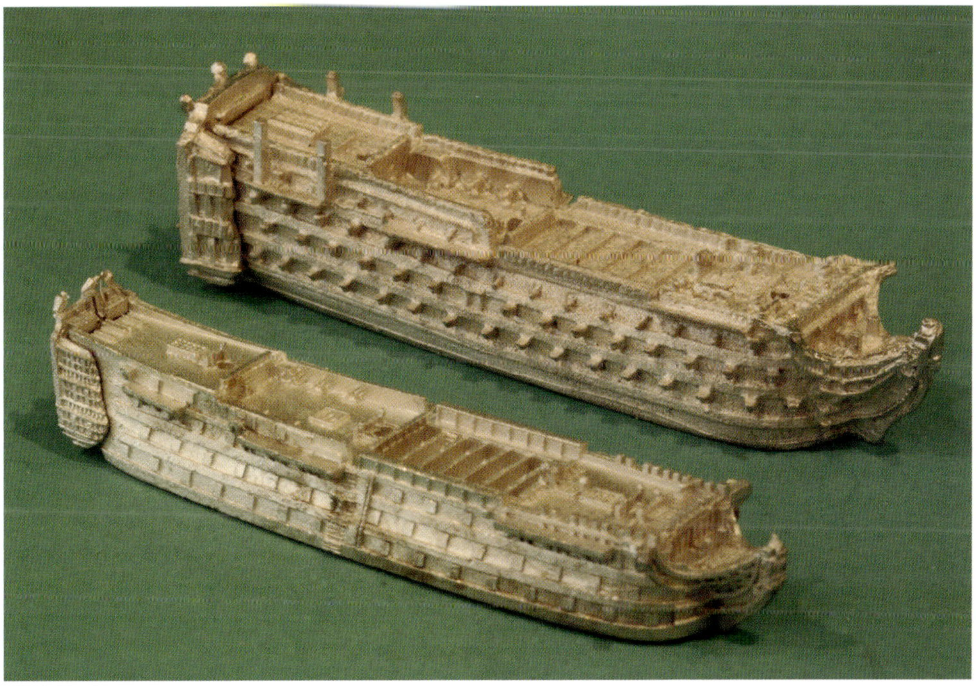

Seen side by side, both miniatures are instantly recognisable as *Victory* and Langton's robust detailing eases painting, open gun ports, wide selection of sail sets provide versatility for the gamer and modeller. GHQ's model has very fine detail that suits the scale enthusiast. Despite being modelled to 1:1200 (2½in long), the models are noticeably different in actual size and style, but that is not really an issue unless you are mixing models between the two ranges.

HENRY TURNER *VICTORY* 1765

1:700 Scale

Henry Turner's *Victory* is the only kit available in her pre-1800 refit appearance with open stern galleries and elaborate figurehead. No physical model is actually sold, just the files (*.stl* or *.obj* format files) to download and resin-print at home. With resin printing the model is built up in layers and that allows for the waist to be fully hollowed out with detailed cannons poking out through *open* gun ports. Lattice work of

all kinds are printed fully hollow. The model is exquisitely detailed and only the unrealistic deck planking detail requires filling for a scale effect. If you have 3D modelling skills, the files can be modified to correct the deck planking before printing. Generic sail sets are also available for downloading, but a better option is to scratch build these to match the finesse of the hull.

MERIDIAN TRAFALGAR RANGE *VICTORY* 1:700 Scale

This is the original Skytrex white metal kit now offered by Navy Models & Books. The hull is cast in resin with the masts and yards in white metal. The gun ports are modelled open and heightened bulwarks fitted to the forecastle, quarter and poop decks. Covered hammock netting is provided for the ship's waist, and the breaks of the quarterdeck and poop. The hull is finely detailed with a few omissions, but the moulding of some of the gratings are a little indistinct and uneven. Boat beams are a separate part complete with a full suite of ship's boats.

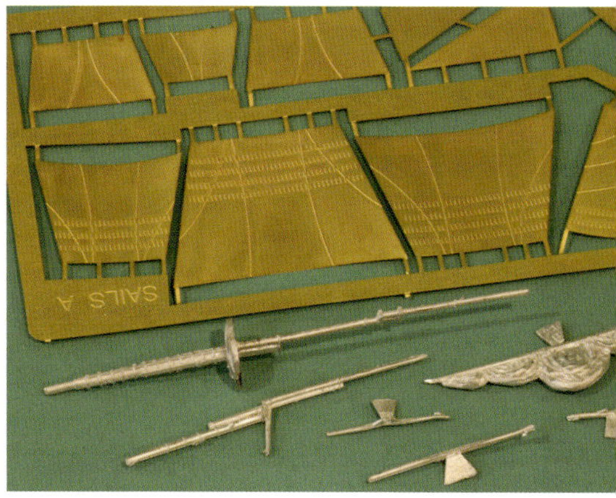

The white metal masts and yards are scale-like. Being white metal, they are stiff enough to take some tension from the rigging. No stunsail booms are included and would have to be added from brass rod if desired. The etch brass shrouds and ratlines are very fine, but over-scale in order to make them robust. They are simply glued to the moulded channels on the hull and to the top of the mast with no deadeye detail that is noticeable in this scale. The fore and main yards are moulded with realistically modelled furled sails. Full courses are to be made of paper or optional etch brass ones purchased and fitted. The kit instructions are generic but the rigging instructions are quite complete in describing how to fit some realistic representative rigging following typical British, French, and Spanish practices. This kit provides the robustness required for a wargame model and a great start for a scale model for display.

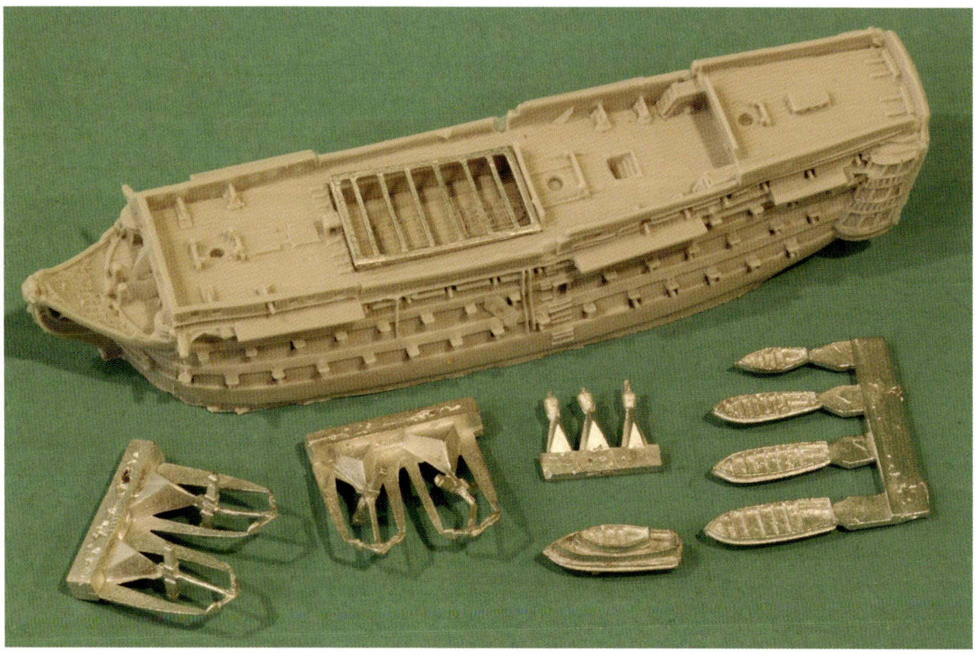

ARTIST HOBBY **HMS *VICTORY*** 1:700 Scale

For the scale enthusiast is Artist Hobby's remarkable resin and brass kit of *Victory* as she appears in Portsmouth today. The kit was designed using CAD and 3D modelling technologies and is precise in virtually all details, so much so the hull decorations, such as the balustrades and window frames are difficult to see without a magnifying glass. The hull portrays the gun ports open and guns run out, and the kit is offered in full or waterline configurations. The moulded decks have fine planking detail and cast cannons on the quarter-deck. The two forecastle carronades and guns are 3D resin-printed on a separate sprue. The deck fittings, like the ship's wheel coamings and gratings, barriers and bitts complete with belaying pins, are provided as tiny photo-etched brass components to be folded up. This material also provides the hammock nettings for the forecastle, waist and poop decks, but the hammocks themselves will have to be made from tiny rolls of two-part epoxy putty. The waist is cut out with boat skids provided in thin strips of photo-etched brass that do not give the impression that these items were hefty beams and are best replaced with square section plastic rod. The gun port lids are relief-etched with hinge detail. No ship's boats are included but these can be taken from 1:700 accessory sprues from plastic kits, and oddly, the three stern lanterns are not provided.

Where the kit really shines is in the portrayal of the masting and rigging. Several lengths of brass rod are provided to solder together or glued up with miniscule photo-etch collars and rings. The ratlines, shrouds, deadeyes detail and the hull channels are provided in a stunningly delicate PE brass that are custom-etched to fit each mast. The fighting tops are also provided as fold up etched brass parts with full detail on the top and bottom faces with the futtock and upper shrouds, ratlines and deadeyes as a single part. Also included are etched footropes for the yards, and backstays for the masts. These are very delicate and flat, and replacing them with thread or wire would yield a more pleasing effect. Printed sails are provided on a cream coloured paper. This remarkable kit pushes the limit on scale fidelity – to the point that is will be a very difficult model to build, but one that will stand out in a collection of 1:700 ships to show the evolution of the Senior Service over time.

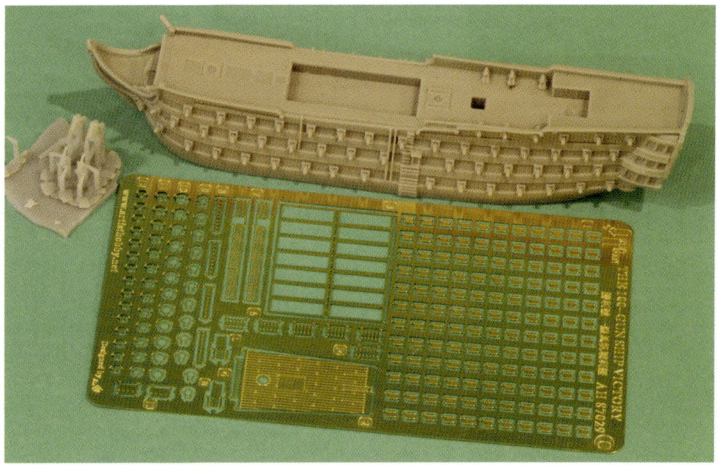

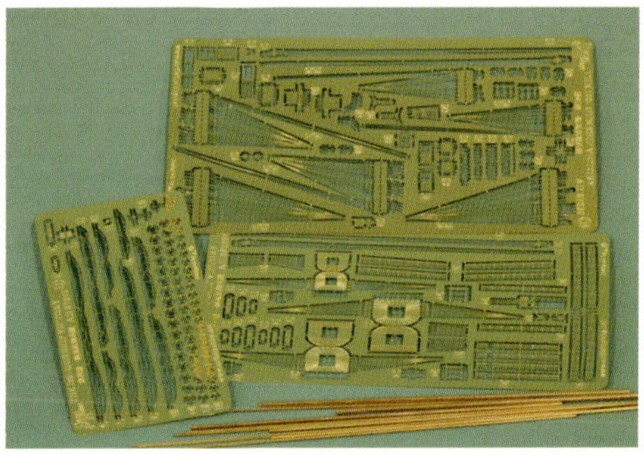

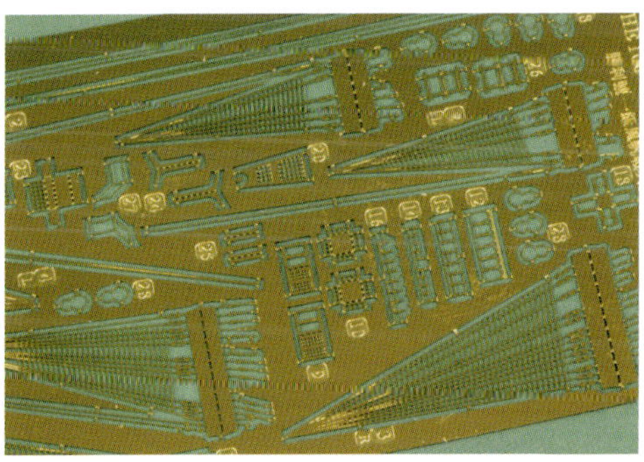

The design approach for these three kits could not be more different and each caters to the wargamer (Black Sea's range), the scale modeller (Artist Hobby) with the Meridian kit falling in between. The Artist Hobby kit captures *Victory*'s hull lines perfectly owing to the 3D modelling processes to create the master, whereas the other two kits are noticeably chunkier but the details being much more distinct will be easier to paint and shade and highlight. The Warlord Games model is toy-like in its detailing and execution, but should be no obstacle to a dedicated modeller to refine. The Meridian kit is the most authentic for *Victory* at Trafalgar, and an exceptional model would result by cross kitting the Artist Hobby masting and rigging components to the Meridian hull and details.

WARLORD GAMES' BLACK SEA RANGE
HMS *VICTORY* 1:700 Scale

The box contains all the elements for the ship to join a game played by the Black Sea's ruleset. The model itself is cast resin and white metal; sails, flags and a false sea are printed on paper; includes a spool of rigging thread; and interestingly the shrouds and ratlines printed on clear acetate sheet. The resin hull is robustly detailed with white metal stern galleries. The ship's deck is detailed with overly wide and short planks, disappointing to gamers and scale enthusiasts alike, but can be filled and de-emphasised with filler. The forecastle and poop bulwarks are modelled with low bulwarks topped with hammock nettings.

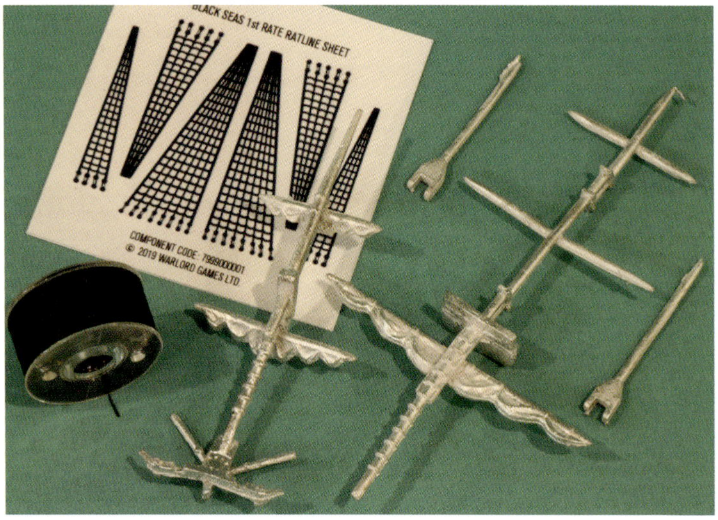

The masts and yards are cast in a single part, and the fore and main yards feature furled sails. The lower masts are detailed with cheeks and hoops, with the fighting tops and caps moulded in place. Oddly, the lower, upper, and topgallant masts have unusual proportions. The lower mast, normally the thickest is actually narrower than the upper mast, and the topgallant as thick as the upper mast. The bowsprit also suffers from the same problem being narrower than the jibboom, and the casting is also missing the flying jibboom. The yards are strangely proportioned as well, with the upper yard being about as long as the main yard. No studdingsail booms are included.

Shrouds, ratlines and deadeyes are provided as printed lines on clear acetate but it may have worked better if the shrouds and the ratlines were not printed to the same thickness. The full sails are die-cut in fully coloured card that can be used as patterns for sails cut from painted copy paper for a finer effect. Finally, the kit comes with a generic set of nicely printed flags and pennants.

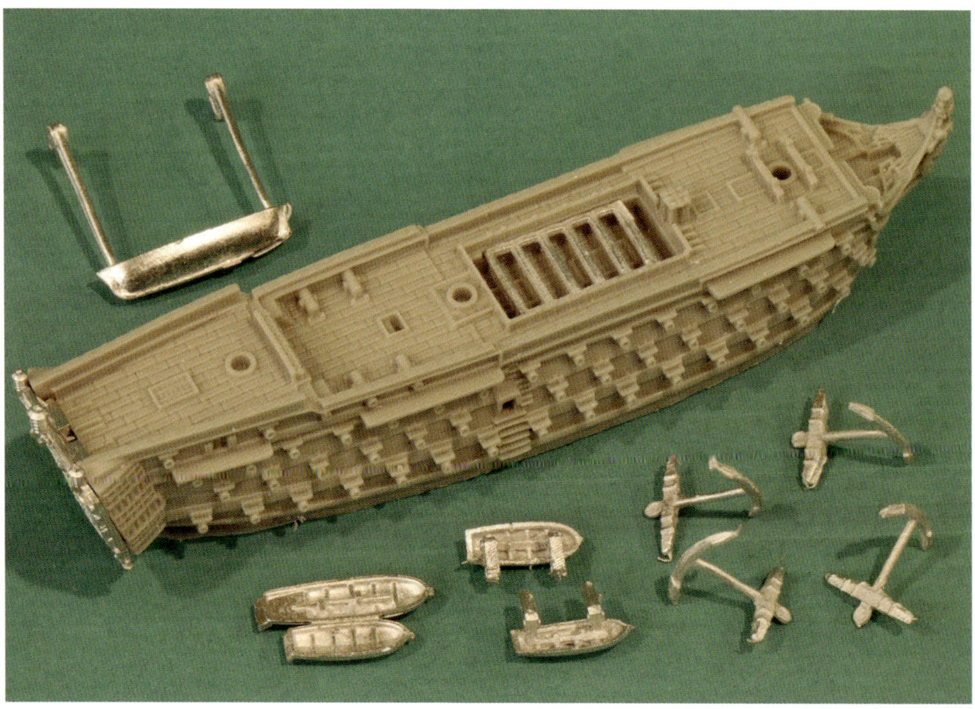

AIRFIX **HMS *VICTORY*** STARTER SET Indeterminate Scale

The first plastic kit of *Victory* ever manufactured was released in 1959. As a representation of *Victory*, the kit just broadly (even at that, kind of) resembles the ship. The hull details are heavy, and the deck details are imaginary. Masts and billowing sails are separately moulded parts to appeal to younger modellers and it remains so to this day. The kit contains a decal sheet with printed decoration for the galleries and windows. A few flags are included but the all-important St George's Cross on the White Ensign wasn't printed correctly. Nevertheless, this is a wonderful kit for a younger modeller, especially with the included paint, glue and brush that will allow them to refight Trafalgar with the greatest tool they have – their imagination.

REVELL **HMS *VICTORY*** 1:450 Scale

This kit allows a full hull or waterline model to be constructed. The upper hull mouldings carry fine detail, and this is the only kit whose inner bulwarks are detailed with kevel blocks and decorative mouldings. All of the bulwarks are low representing her restored appearance and are bereft of hammock netting detail. The underwater hull is of the correct shape but unfortunately detailed with heavily engraved lines to represent the individual copper plates in a wholly unrealistic way. Each row of hull plates should be staggered in a brickwork pattern but represented with parallel horizontal and vertical lines.

The stern gallery is a delightful moulding with all of the carved detail, and a decal is provided to go over the top of them to simplify painting. The deck moulding is a mix of fine detail and clunky simplification.

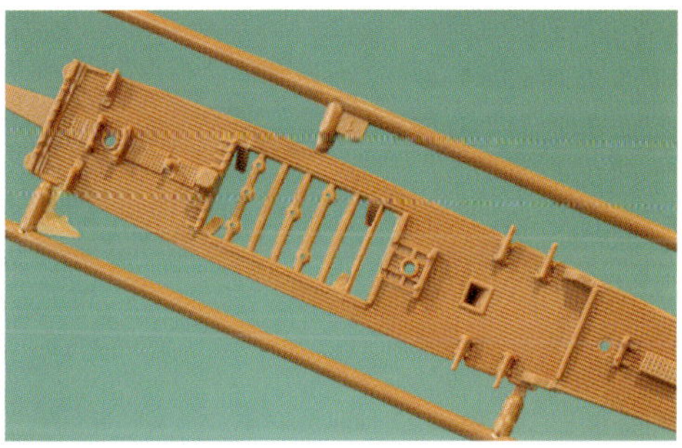

For example, the boat beams are heavily moulded with large locating lugs for the ship's boats and the deck planking detail is crude. However, the carronades and guns moulded in place are well done; but the bitts, barricades, and belfry are moulded solid integrally with the deck.

The masts, fighting tops and yards are moulded together as single units. They are

very fine and prone to bending out of shape easily under the slightest strain of rigging. Ratlines, shrouds and deadeyes are provided in a single heavy moulding, and the sails are thick and devoid of any detail. Overall, this kit is a mix of fine detail and gross oversimplification. The scale enthusiast will find much potential in the hull mouldings, but much of the rest is better off being made from scratch to match its overall finesse.

AIRFIX **HMS *VICTORY*** 1:180 Scale

This kit has been continuously available since 1965. Although the kit is emblazoned *HMS Victory 1765*, the ship is definitely not the open stern version of her as built. The year refers to the launching date and the kit itself represents her 1950s restored 'near Trafalgar' appearance in Portsmouth. The kit appears to be based on plans found in C Nepean Longridge's classic 1961 book *The Anatomy of Nelson's Ships* drawn by George F Campbell. The hull halves are delicately detailed with carvings and mouldings, and the copper

plating on the hull is rendered in the correct pattern. In contrast, the hull planking is represented by heavily engraved lines, but the wales feature proper 'anchor stock' planking pattern with fine raised lines. The side and stern galleries are finely detailed that are proud enough to be easily picked out with a fine paint brush. There are a few detail errors, such as missing stools for the backstays, and the number of chain plates moulded on the hull sides do not match the number of deadeyes; nor are they entirely symmetrical on the port and starboard sides.

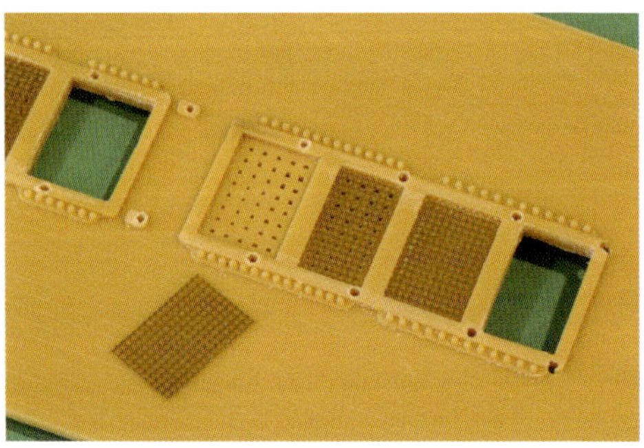

Etched brass screen used to cover up the poorly moulded gratings.

The deck planking is represented by fine raised lines that are marred with a few sinkholes. The hatch coamings are filled with thick gratings that are moulded in place, and the deck barricades are moulded solid. The quarterdeck panelling and screens are provided as separate parts. The ship's boats are clean mouldings and include oars and separate rudders.

The lower masts are detailed mouldings and robust enough to take the strain of

The kit hull assembled with decks in place and detailed.

rigging but the topmasts and topgallants are very thin and easily pulled out of shape and should be replaced with scratch-built substitutes in wood or brass rod. The bowsprit is robust but the jibboom and flying jibboom should be replaced with something stiffer. No studdingsail booms are included.

Shrouds and ratlines are constructed on a loom over which thread of different thicknesses (the kit supplied thread is too thick and coarse and should be replaced) are wound and coated with PVA. The loom works remarkably well and can be kept for other models. The rigging diagram provided in the instructions is very basic and confusing. The vacform plastic sails are nicely detailed, thin, and moulded with a realistic 'hang'. Alternatively, they can serve as a pattern for replacements made from painted paper. No stunsails as fitted at Trafalgar are included.

The Airfix kit is one of the best renditions of the ship in plastic, and its size (the hull, not including the bowsprit) is, at 15¼in in length, large enough to be easily built, displayed and detailed without being too fiddly. If you can find a copy, the first of Airfix's 'Classic Ships' series of books, *HMS Victory* by Noel C Hackney, provides extensive rigging instructions, and a host of other detail improvements to the kit. Bear in mind that the book is a product of its time, and many modelmaking products common today would make some of his methods obsolete.

Kit mast and yards with brass and wood replacements for strength.

View of waist. The covered hammock nettings were made from scratch and added to the hull.

The completed Airfix kit in harbour rig with scratch-built details.

REVELL HMS *VICTORY* 1:225 Scale

This kit has been widely available since the early 1960s. The hull castings have very fine raised lines to represent the planking, and the wales show the authentic 'anchor stock' planking. The rendition of the copper plating is superb. The plates show the proper staggered pattern, but also how each plate overlapped the one behind it complete with delicate nail head detail. The side gallery windows and carvings are very fine but the side steps are over-thick. The bulwarks are low and no hammock nettings provided. The stern transom is beautifully detailed but marred with large placement lugs for the boat davits and lanterns that impinge on the carved decoration. The figurehead is very well detailed, as are the bow cheeks.

The decks feature fine planking detail with a simulated wood-grain appearance that will delight or annoy some modellers. In a bid for detail, several randomly placed coils of rope are moulded to the deck that would get a fellow a rap of the bosun's rattan. The upper gun deck has the gun carriages moulded to the deck. There are no quarterdeck screens (they would have been struck below when beating to quarters) and the large lugs that hold up the poop deck are visible through the gap between decks. The bitts, barricades, and belfry are separate parts and the rails have belaying pins moulded into them. The forecastle and quarterdeck guns are nicely detailed parts. Empty ship's boats are provided for the

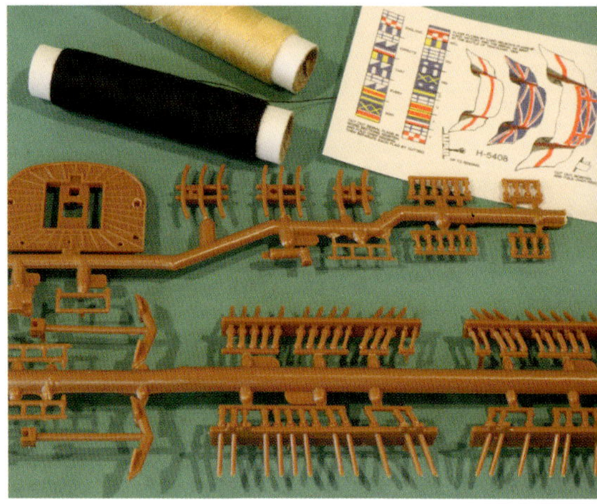

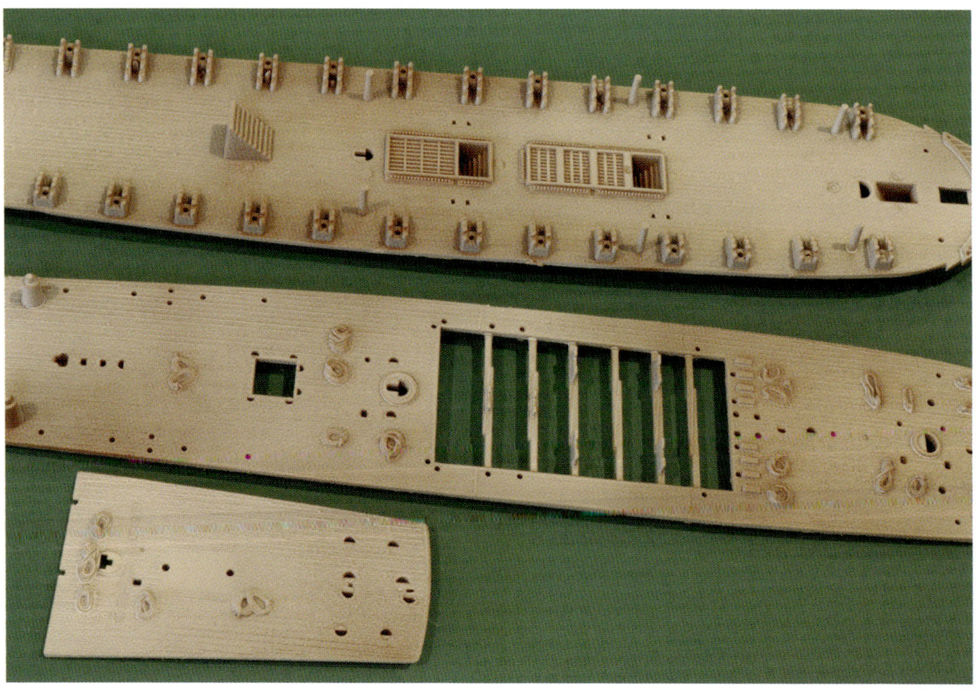

Parts primed white for clarity.

davits and boat beams. Some scratch-built oars and casks would detail them out nicely.

The lower and upper masts can be used out of the box, and each is very well detailed with bands and cheeks, but the main mast suffers from sink holes. The yards and booms are slender and prone to bend under rigging. The bowsprit is stout but the jibboom should be replaced, and a flying jibboom needs to be added. No stunsail booms or sails are included. When it comes to the rigging, the shrouds and ratlines are heavily moulded plastic items but the channels and deadeyes are delicately moulded and sport clear lanyard detail between the upper and lower deadeyes. Nicely detailed vacformed sails round off the kit contents.

The painting instructions are nominally for *Victory*'s Trafalgar appearance, but they are odd and should not be followed. The kit box shows the built-up model in the familiar black and yellow scheme, but the colour strakes are placed incorrectly, and contradict the kit instructions that says paint the yellow strakes white. The kit includes a sheet of paper flags with the 'England Expects...' signal, but they are definitely not in Popham's code and should not be used.

HELLER **HMS *VICTORY*** 1:100 Scale

When released in 1979 this kit was the largest plastic ship kit available (2107 parts) and has yet to be eclipsed. The hull castings are unusual in that the side entry ports are replaced with gun ports as shown on single model of *Victory* (F2881) in the National Maritime Museum at Greenwich. The model scores in providing well represented hull and deck planking and virtually all fittings as separate parts. The guns are nicely rendered on multi-part carriages complete with quoins. The belfry, bitts, companionways and quarterdeck screens are well detailed; and all of the windows are moulded open and glazed with clear plastic. The carvings and decorations are extremely well done, and small details like rigols and gun port lid lanyard bosses are included. The ship's name is moulded within a small cartouche. The weakest aspect of the hull is the representation of the copper plating below the waterline. It is

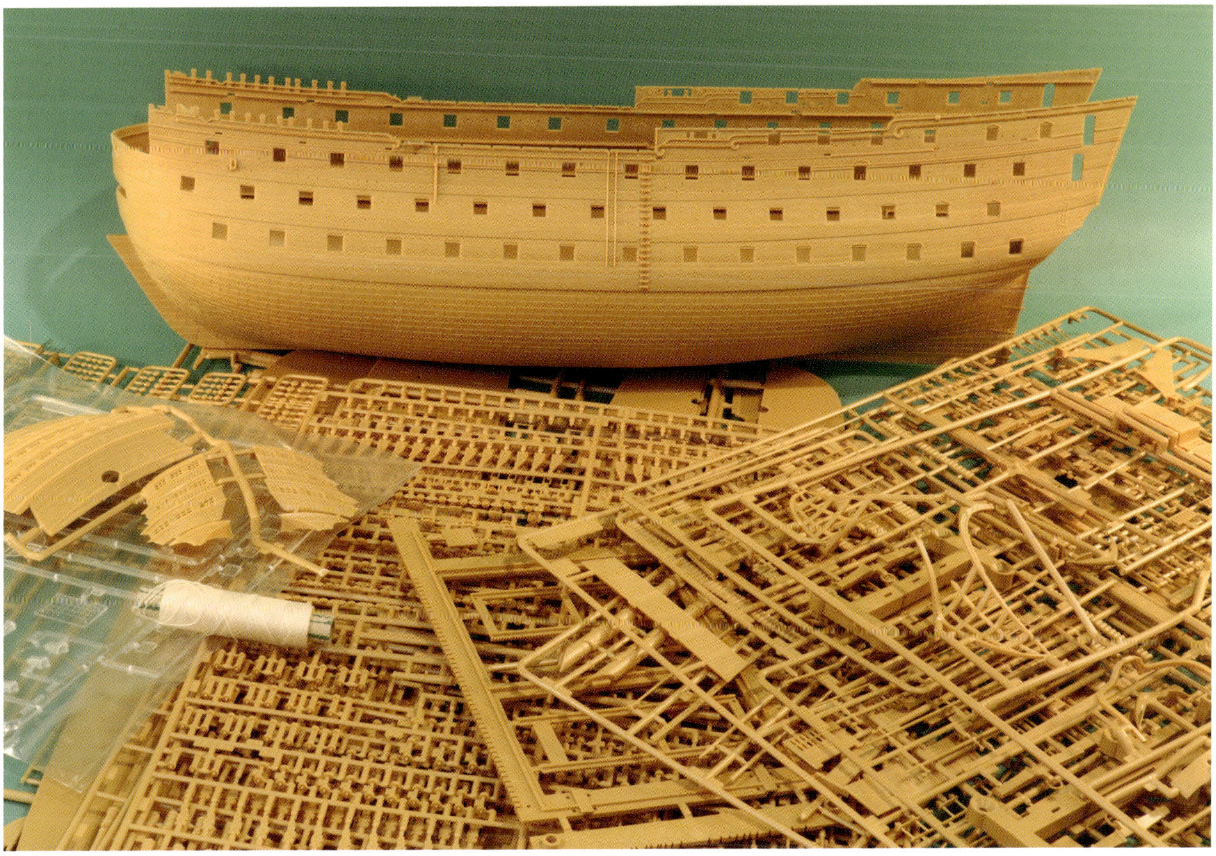

undetailed and worst of all, it is incomplete.

All of the planking is engraved with 'wood-grain' textures, and the main wales feature well defined engraved anchor-stock planking detail. The gratings are moulded unrealistically flat and all hatches and coamings are too low. The ship's boats are large and open and cry out for framing detail on the interior from plastic strip.

Given the large scale of the model, the plastic hull is too thin. The sides of a First Rate were very thick and this is apparent though open gun ports. If modelling the ports open, each opening on the lower and main gun deck should be lined with square section plastic strip to simulate the thickness. This is not required on the upper gun deck because the plastic hull is just about thick enough for this area.

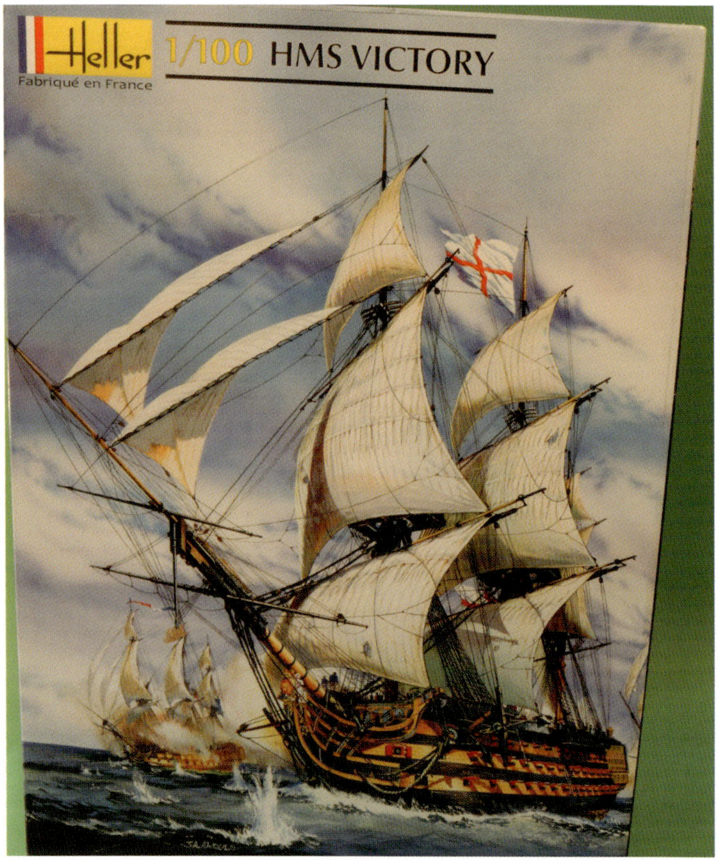

In this scale, the model is readily rigged like the actual ship with blocks and deadeyes that are seized and pulled taut that will put stress on the masts and yards. Luckily, because the lower and top masts, and the fore and main lower yards are assembled from two hollow halves, a length of brass rod can be epoxied in place before assembly. The topgallant masts, and remaining yards are moulded to scale which means they are thin and easily bent, and remaking them from wooden dowel sanded to shape is the order of the day. The bowsprit is made of two solid halves and best hollowed to take a length of brass rod for strength. The jib and flying jibboom should be replaced with items from brass rod or shaped wooden dowel.

The kit provides a loom for shrouds and ratlines and separate plastic deadeyes pierced for lanyards. However, the chains and chain plates are represented inauthentically with single lengths of thread instead of oval shaped chain links. The kit provides hundreds of single, double and treble rigging blocks that broadly resemble the

real items, as well as several spools of thread in different sizes but it is nowhere near the right number of sizes actually required. Sails are provided as vacuformed plastic, and stunsail booms and sails are included.

The Heller kit provides a superlative basis for a truly authentic model of *Victory*. The kit is in the same scale as many wooden kits of this ship, and many of the fittings from wooden kits, such as belaying pins, gratings, eyebolts, blocks, cleats, copper plating, strops and chain and chain plates can replace the flimsy or inauthentic plastic items. Similarly, many items from this kit are done far better than the generic items found in some wooden kits, and many items such as the ship's guns and carriages, carvings and other detail parts can be used to provide scale fidelity to these kits. Heller's model allows you to get the best of both modelling genres.

Wooden Kits

Virtually every wooden ship kit manufacturer offers a *Victory*. It makes sense to modellers that wooden ships should be made of wood, and working in wood brings about a satisfaction that doesn't exist in other mediums. However, modellers should be aware that most wooden kits are designed as decorative models that are unpainted to allow the beauty of the exotic hardwoods used in the model's construction to show. These kits also gild and polish the metal parts where in reality, they would have been blackened. In contrast, an authentic model attempts to replicate the actual finish of the ship by painting in the correct colours. In many cases, a decorative model is accurate in form and details, and can be made authentic by finishing in correct colour schemes, planking the deck to scale, or remaking some fittings.

In wooden kits, shaped bulkheads are glued transversely to a profile of the hull called the *false keel* to form a framework that is planked over with wood strips or shaped pieces of thin plywood. This construction is called *plank on bulkhead* and the framework is planked over once or twice. Most kits are planked twice, first in a softwood like lime to create the basic hull carcass, followed by a second layer in a thin hardwood like walnut. The advantage of double-plank on bulkhead models is that the first layer allows you to shape the hull and correct any dips or bumps before planking over a second time which shows off the run of the planking defining the beauty of *Victory*'s lines. Single-planked kits are more difficult because you only get one chance to get the planking correct when the wood wants to dip in between bulkheads.

Wooden kit manufacturers often provide fittings from a generic pool that are neither entirely correct nor in scale with the kit. Better kits provide custom sets of cast and etched brass fittings specific to *Victory*. All kits provide wood stock in different sizes to be cut, slotted and shaped according to the kit drawings. Be aware that a lot of the details or shapes shown on the kit plans are sized to utilise generic parts or wood stock and are not to scale. Masts and yards are shaped from dowels, and rigging line must often be dyed the correct colour. A helpful reference to building and detailing wooden kits is this author's *Ship Models from the Age of Sail: Building and Enhancing Commercial Kits*. Also highly recommended is membership of the US-based *Nautical Research Guild*, whose website and publications feature extensive reviews and build logs of many hundreds of wooden kits.

CALDERCRAFT **HMS *VICTORY*** 1:72 Scale

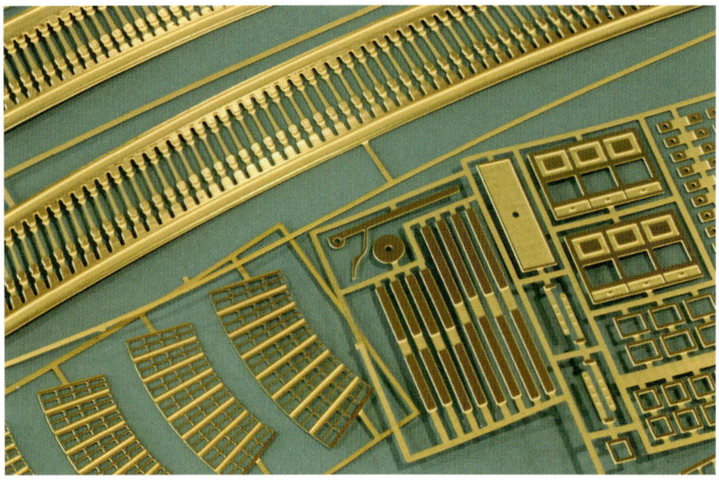

Of all the wooden kits of *Victory* extant, this kit is the best in terms of quality of the wood, custom fittings, carvings, and sheets of etched brass details covering thousands of items. The kit supplies multiple spools of high-quality linen rigging cord, a huge set of plans and three instruction booklets. The biggest weakness of the kit is that the hundreds of rigging blocks are generic items that bear only a passing resemblance to blocks – but can be replaced at an added expense. The research used to develop the model has been reviewed by the Curator of the *HMS Victory* Museum in Portsmouth ensuring the kit features represent the latest information. The model was designed to portray

Victory in her 1805 appearance with heightened bulwarks at the forecastle, quarterdeck and poop, but can be built with the lower bulwarks as she looks today. The huge box is literally filled to the brim

WOODEN KITS (ALPHABETICAL BY MANUFACTURER)

Manufacturer	Scale	Construction	Type
Amati	1:64	Double PoB	Authentic
Artesania Latina	1:84	Single PoB	Decorative

This kit is out of production, but is still found in many shops. A simplified model of *Victory* with many out-of-scale fittings. An upgraded version is available from DeAgostini as a monthly part work.

Billings	1:75	Double PoB	Semi-Authentic

Generally accurate, simplified in many areas. Hull below main wale is single planked, above main wales double planked. No main or middle gun deck provided and guns for these decks are provided as stubs glued into a shallow recess in hull planking. Fittings are in wood, injection-moulded plastic, brass, white metal. No copper plating supplied for underwater hull.

Caldercraft	1:72	Double PoB	Authentic

Accurate and detailed, it incorporates latest research validated by curator of *HMS Victory* Museum, with all items to scale. Most fittings are custom-made for the kit in white metal, etched brass, wood, brass and copper. The kit provides option of fitting barriers to poop and forecastle decks. Copper plates for hull bottom are to scale but feature heavy dimpled patterns to represent the nails. These dimples can be flattened down with a small hammer. One of the very best kits and represents great value for the money and is of a size that is impressive without being too overwhelming. All parts are CNC-cut, so no laser charring to clean off. Highly recommended.

Constructo	1:94	Single PoB	Decorative

Simplified large scale model. Generic, simplified out of scale fittings. Looks like *Victory* at a distance, but less so upon close inspection.

Corel	1:98	Double PoB	Decorative

Generally accurate with nicely detailed plans. Pressed wood fibre for carvings and gratings, inauthentic cast gun port frames. Many fittings are generic but generally to scale. No copper plates supplied for hull bottom. Has been used as basis for accurate and authentic model with extensive scratch building.

Corel	1:98	Midship cross section	Decorative

The exposed ship frames are stylised and do not accurately represent how *Victory*'s frames were constructed. The model is 'cutaway' to give a general representation of *Victory*'s interior amidships. The kit serves as a good basis for an accurate cutaway model, but work showing the bilge waterways for example will have to be made from scratch and with reference to authentic plans. Complete main mast with rigging (shrouds and ratlines) are provided.

DeAgostini	1:84	Single PoB	Decorative

Part work kit purchased monthly as part of a magazine subscription. Likely an upgraded Artesania Latina kit. Some fittings to scale and others not, planking definitely not to scale. No copper plates included for underwater hull. Kit includes figures of Nelson and crew for the decks. Each step of the partwork is accompanied by excellent illustrated construction guide.

DeAgostini	1:72	Midship cross section	Semi-authentic

Part work kit purchased monthly as part of a magazine subscription. This kit provides more authentic midship framing with laser-cut futtocks and scarph joints. The main mast is just a stub. Generally accurate with highly detailed instructions.

Mamoli	1:325	Solid Hull	Decorative

This is a 'beginner' kit with a solid wooden hull to be shaped. The wooden model is highly simplified given the small scale and uses coloured stickers for the carved decorations.

Mamoli	1:90	Double PoB	Decorative

Interesting design that sets cast metal gun ports into the first planking to create depth. Well-shaped metal guns and neatly shaped carriages. Fittings are generic and largely out of scale but general dimensions and shapes accurate. This old kit has been the basis of some superb models with extensive scratch building. The Mamoli brand has been taken over by Dusek Model Ships who have been extensively upgrading the old kits. Perhaps one day an upgraded *Victory* will be released.

Mantua	1:98	Double PoB	Decorative

A very old kit design and now long obsolete. Relies on flat etched brass for round carvings. Gun ports are provided as frames. Turned brass gun barrels are incorrect shape, carriages over large and wholly the wrong shape. Few fittings items or deck planking to scale. No copper plates for underwater hull.

Mantua	1:200	Single PoB	Authentic

Small scale wooden planked kit. Features a lot of photo-etch for decoration, laser-cut and etched deck sheets, copper plating of coloured wood included. A miniature version of a large-scale wooden kit with concessions to scale. High level of detail has been incorporated using laser cutting and etching on deck and hull parts. Part locations are laser-etched into the parts. Guns and carriages not quite the correct shape. Full masting and simplified rigging is also included. This kit provides the basis for highly detailed small scale wooden model.

Panart	1:78	Double PoB	Decorative

Relies heavily on flat etch for relief carvings, poor metal castings for some carvings, generally all items out of scale. Long obsolete.

Panart	1:78	Bow cross section	Semi-Authentic

Stylised framing, representation fine detail including iron knees, partial fore mast and bowsprit. Generally accurate. The headwork is well detailed and a stub of a bowsprit is included. Quite eye-catching when completed out of the box, if extra effort is taken to refine the over-scale parts and planking the model can be rather impressive.

Sergal	1:78	Double PoB	Decorative

There are two kits. Kit #782 contains basic parts. Similar to Panart kit, but decks are laser-etched with a generic planking pattern. No copper plating supplied for underwater hull. Kit #783 includes copper plates for underwater hull and other cast/etched fittings such as an out of scale ship's wheel and binnacle not included in #782. Both long obsolete.

with wood stock weighing in at over 20kg and is remarkable for the massive numbers of prefabricated CNC [computer numerical control] wooden parts. Each kit has a unique serial number and registering your kit with the manufacturer will ensure that as new research that affects a part is uncovered on the ship you will receive any update or a new part. The completed model has an overall length (bowsprit to taffrail) 1385mm (54.5in), 940mm height (37in), and 525mm (21.6in) width.

Unique framing design for the hull and gunports. *(Photo used with permission by Christopher Watton)*

AMATI **HMS *VICTORY*** 1:64 Scale

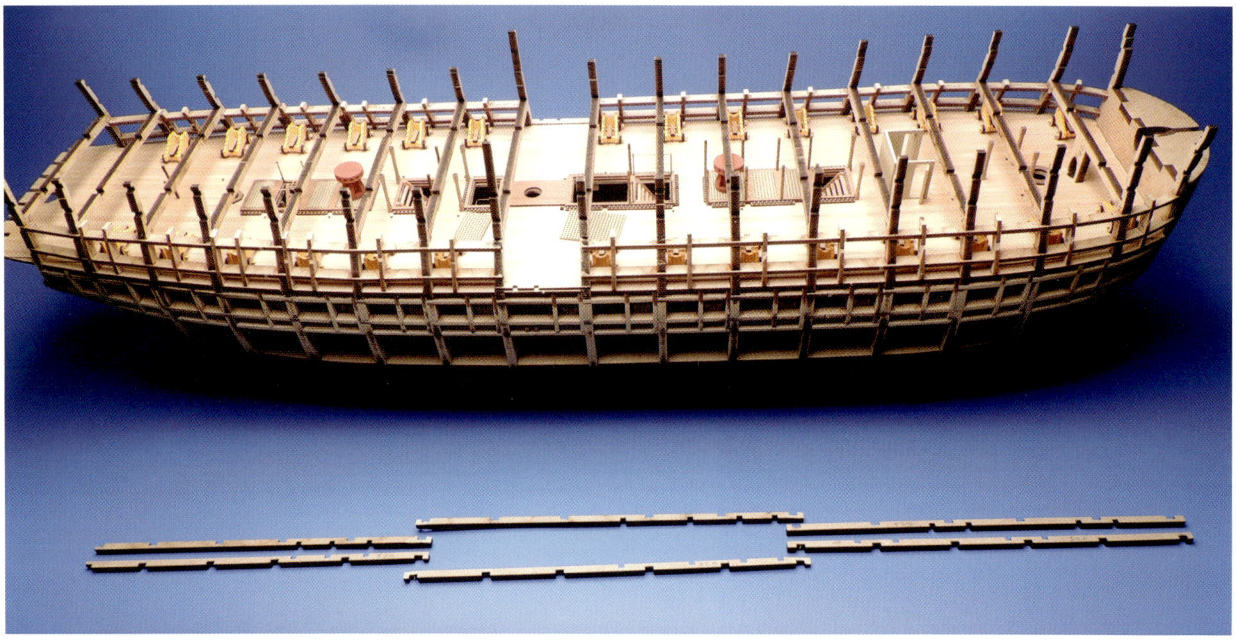

The stern galleries are fully framed to accommodate the windows. *(Photo used with permission by Christopher Watton)*

This soon-to-be-released gigantic kit will be the ultimate model of *Victory* with the low bulwarks. Designed by Vanguard Models' Chris Watton, this kit has incorporated the latest innovations in wooden kit design and to be as modeller-friendly as possible. Innovative touches, such as the framing of gun ports into the hull framework is the first of its kind that will eliminate much of the tedium of fitting individual linings and sills. A great deal of research and care to create scale components is a hallmark of the design. This venerable Italian brand is known for producing high quality kits and this will one will rank amongst the largest kits ever produced.

Accessories

Accessories for *Victory* come in two forms – items created for specific kits like Airfix's 1:180 and Heller's 1:100 scale kits, or generic items suitable for any model.

SCALEDECKS *VICTORY* WOODEN DECK 1:180 Scale

Scaledecks offer a set of printed wood veneers that perfectly cover the Airfix kit decks. The veneer is not self-adhesive and is fixed with polyurethane or epoxy glue. This product is unusual in that the veneer is printed over with scale planking detail, and each plank artfully coloured a different shade of tan and greyish brown. The overprinting does cover up much of the veneer's natural grain pattern yielding a perfectly scaled effect, but the colours are a bit garish and best toned down with a thin overspray of light grey.

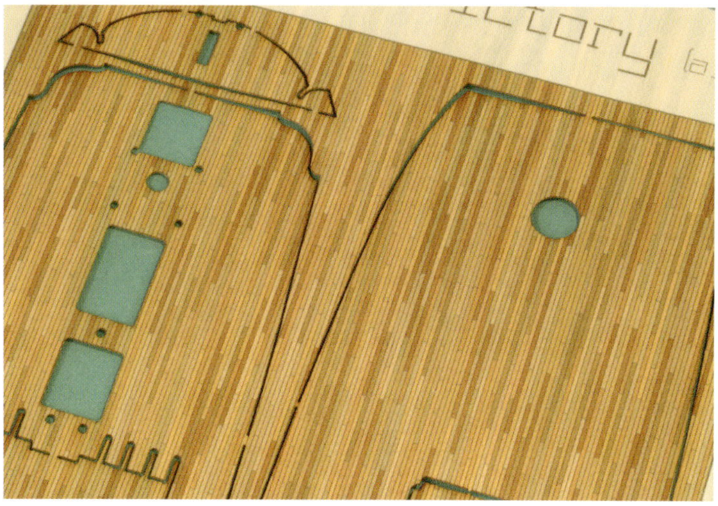

SCALE WARSHIP *VICTORY* ETCH AND 3D PRINTED ACCESSORIES 1:180 and 1:100 Scales

Scale Warship's brass etch sets tackle some of the most difficult areas of the Airfix and Heller kits. For the Airfix kit, the kit's solidly moulded stern and side galleries windows can be opened up with PE 0109 to fit perfectly scaled window frames. This set also includes deck gratings that drop into place, bowsprit netting, belaying pin racks and skylights. Set 0104 provides a beautifully etched shroud, ratline and deadeye detail complete with lanyards and chain plates. Set 0099 provides all of *Victory*'s hammock netting. These etch parts are folded up and you can fill them with rolled hammocks made from A+B putty.

To aid with the rigging, several sets of 3D printed blocks, cleats, kevel bitts, and

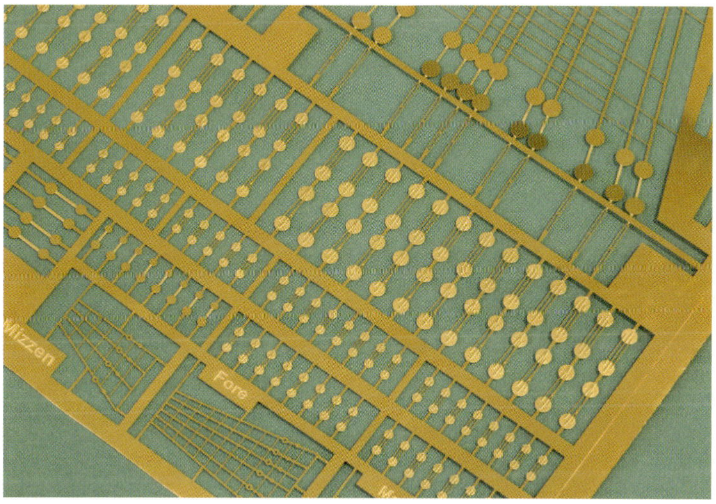

Ratline, shroud, deadeye and chainplate details (PE 0104).

Victory's windows, gratings and hull details (PE 0109).

Hammock nettings for Airfix's kit (PE 0099).

Right: 3D printed details parts such as mouldings and bitts.

hearts are offered. Being in scale, these items are very small and rigging them will be a fun challenge. Also available are a set of deck bitts and forecastle beakhead rails to replace the heavily moulded kit items. Set 0164 is a generic set of mast and yard fittings suitable for models from 1:130 to 1:180 scale. This sets provides plenty of eyebolts, cleats, long eyebolts for rigging footropes and jackstays among other common items found on sailing ships. It is recommended to have a couple of sheets on hand as you never seem to have enough eyebolts, and these items are far more in scale than twisted wire ones usually sold in model shops.

For Heller's 1:100 scale kit, there are two sets that can be applied to the kit – or useful on any 1:96 to 1:100 scale wooden ship. Set 0107 provides a complete set of chains and chain plates. This most useful set allows the chain plate detail to be rendered authentically in scale. With this set you do not have to form wire and solder the various links together, or rely on thread. The parts can be snipped, assembled and any joints held closed with a merest dab of cyanoacrylate glue. Set CAMB 96042 provides a generic set of eyebolts, hooks and rings. It is one of those bread and butter sets that you will be using several of.

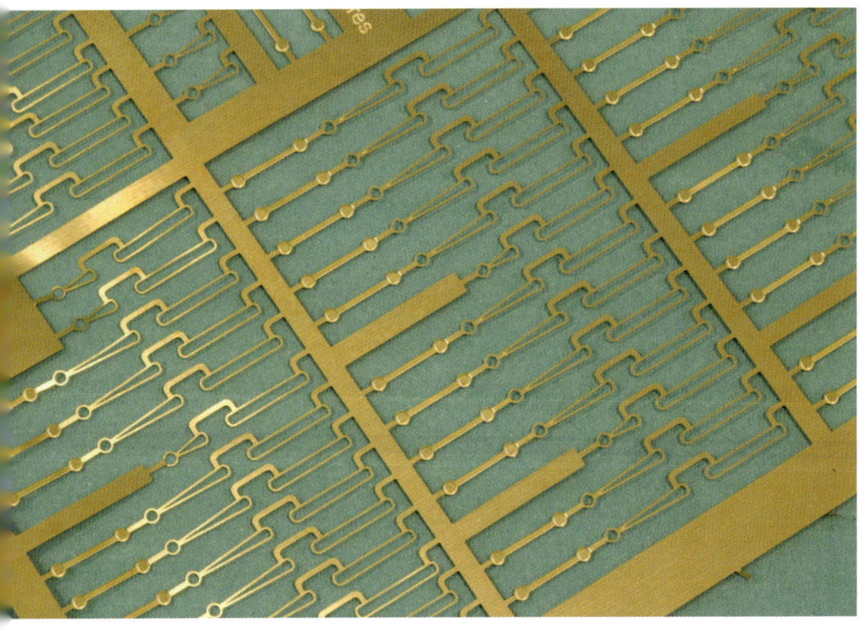

Below: Chainplate details for the Heller kit (PE 0107).

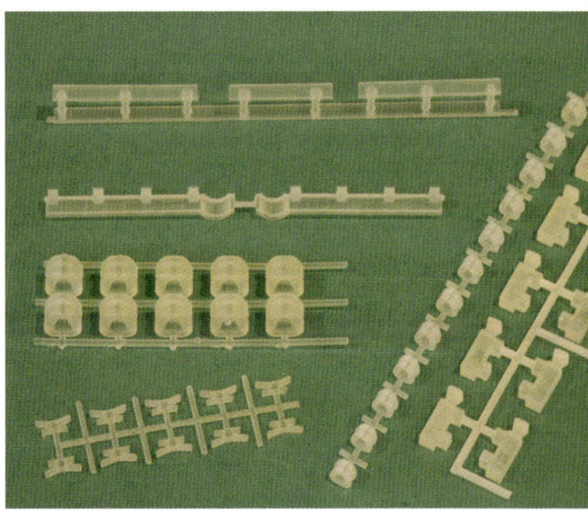

Below right: Rigging blocks in 3D printed plastic.

HISTORIC SHIP MODELS (HiS MODELS) ACCESSORIES

HiS Models sell an extensive range of accessories suitable for any plastic or wooden kit. Offered are complete sets of scaled walnut rigging blocks, wooden decks, and sets of fully sewn fabric sails that are precisely cut or sewn using CNC-based designs that accurately reproduce details down to planking patterns or fabric bolts on sails. HiS Models have produced a number of items for the Airfix, Heller and Revell (1:225) *Victory* kits.

Depending on scale, the sail sets are produced two ways. For the small-scale Airfix and Revell kits the sails are embroidered onto a single piece of fine weave fabric. The sails are carefully cut out, taking care not to cut the stitching around each sail. Prior to cutting, it would be wise to first lightly dye the sails to kill the whiteness of the fabric, and coat them with fabric glue to act as a sizing to prevent fraying. For Heller's *Victory*, each individual sail is cut and sewn using CNC. These sails are beautiful and the fabric weave very fine. Two sets of sails are available, all easy sail and a separate set of studding sails.

The wooden deck overlays are laser-cut and etched with the correct pattern of planks with full trennel detail. The set for the 1:100 *Victory* is cut from several sheets that also includes channels, gratings, and boat beam detail. The officers' cabins are also fully detailed with etched diamond pattern flooring to represent the painted canvas covering. The overlays are provided in oak or beech and your choice depends on your aesthetic preferences. They fit the plastic decks perfectly, and must be glued down using epoxy or a polyurethane glue. The set for the Airfix kit is similar, and the wood grain is not obtrusive but realistic in this small scale.

Rigging sets are a speciality complete

All plain sail for Heller's kit.

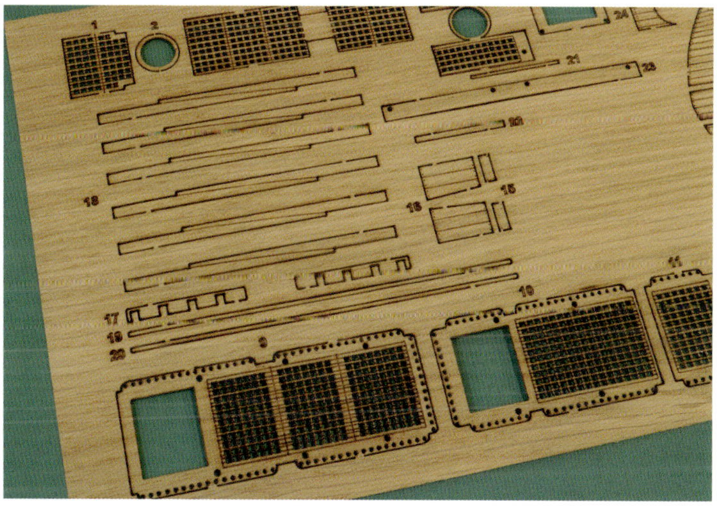

Close up of wooden deck for Heller's *Victory* showing channels, boat beams and gratings.

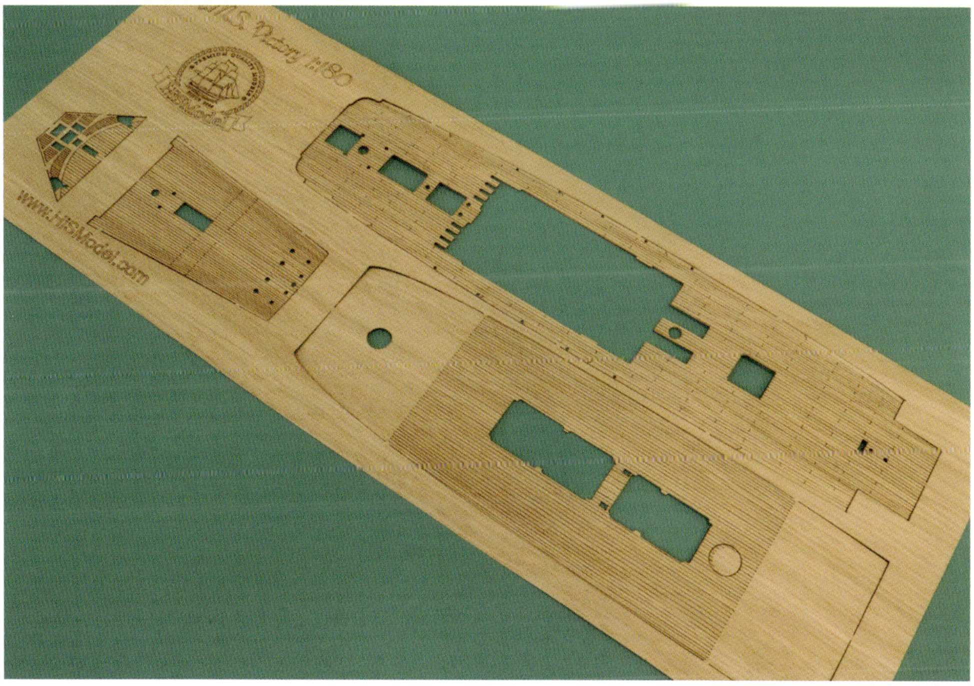

Wooden deck for Airfix's *Victory* in oak.

Right: Rigging set for Airfix's *Victory*. The tiny wooden blocks are shaped like actual blocks found on the full-size ship.

with all wooden rigging blocks, deadeyes and several sizes of thread; they are available for the Airfix or Heller kits. The blocks are laser-cut to look like real blocks (they even offer different blocks of British and French design) and include sheave detail. Some are extremely tiny and a needle threader is required to keep one's sanity intact. Separate sets are available for the standing or the running rigging, and full instruction on which blocks and threads to use is fully detailed on the HiS Model website.

Other useful accessories include sets of turned brass guns and in the larger scales correctly shaped laser carriages to carry them. There are several useful sheets of generic fittings, such as hooks, rings, and eyebolts in a variety of sizes. Mast parrels that allow the yards to be held against the mast are available as sets of beads with blackened etch brass spacers that are threaded together. *Victory*'s flags and pennants sharply printed on fine fabric are available and are a vast improvement on the kit-supplied paper flags.

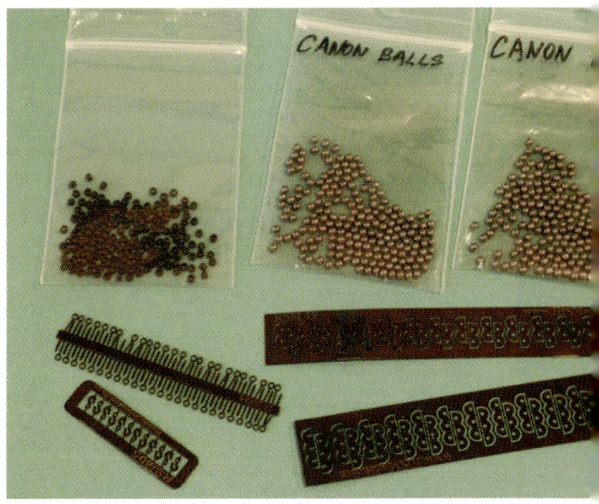

Below, right: Cannon balls, parrel beads and spacers, and eyebolts.

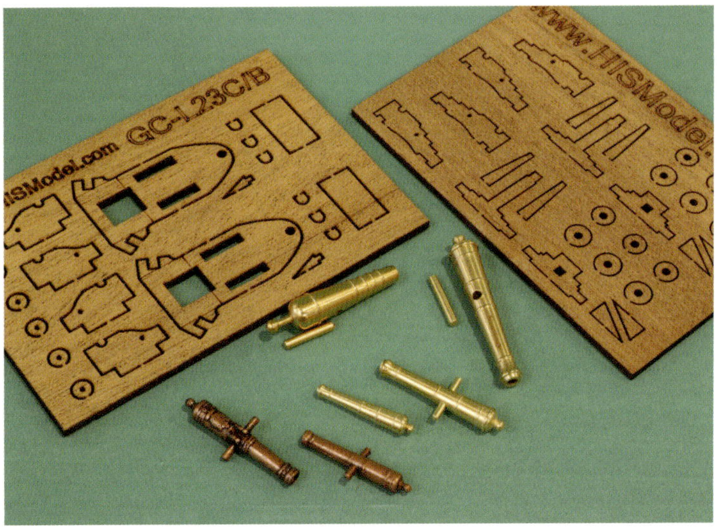

DAFINISMUS **HMS *VICTORY*** FITTINGS 1:100 Scale

Scale etched windows, gunport lid, rigols and hinges.

There are eight sets of etched parts and six sets of resin parts created for Heller's kit. The sheets were designed by a modeller, Daniel Fischer, who intended these parts for his own use and now offers them to others. The designs of the sets are based on items found on *Victory* as she sits in Portsmouth today and the sets replace moulded or missing items, or refine existing details, such as window frames, gratings, gun port lid details, rigols, ringbolts, channel irons, and even lettering. The coverage of the sets is extensive. The resin sets provide new bitts, side steps and hull side entry ports, knightheads, well as alternative stern carvings to replace the incorrect Prince of Wales feathers for her Trafalgar appearance. These sets bring a great deal of delicacy and finesse to the Heller kit or similarly scaled wooden kits alike.

Etched chainplate assemblies and resin side steps.

Etched skylight and hammock cranes.

Paints for Model Making

Jotika's Admiralty Paints provide a range of acrylic paints for brush and airbrushing matched to *Victory* at Portsmouth before repainting in 2015. They dry to an eggshell finish and cover well.

- Black for 'ironwork' (Metal Black AP9106W)
- Black for hull and general fittings (Dull Black AP9105W)
- White (Matt White AP9111W)
- Blue paint (French Blue AP9117W)
- Red ochre for gun ports sills and inside face of lids (Red Ochre AP9116W)
- Yellow ochre (Yellow Ochre AP9115W)
- Copper (Copper, AP9126W)
- Brass and gold (Gold/Brass, AP9125W)
- Brown for wood (Walnut Brown AP9119W)
- Green for ship's boat decoration (Olive Green AP9118W)

For *Victory's* 2015 repainting, Revell's acrylic colour 36135 Flesh is a good match for Pantone NCS S 3020-Y40R for ochre; and 36109 Anthracite matches Pantone NCS S 8500-N for the black strakes as identified by the HMS *Victory* Museum.

SCRATCH-BUILT *VICTORY* 1:300 scale By ETSURO TSUBOI

A special trip was made to Portsmouth from Tokyo during the building of this miniature model (hull length 224mm) to ensure all of the details were correct and as authentic as possible. The model took ten years to complete and required the design of specialised jigs to carve boats, drill out six sizes of deadeyes (ranging 0.8mm to 1.3mm in diameter), and slot gratings from boxwood only 0.25mm thick. Twenty sizes of the rigging lines were made by hand with a miniature ropewalk from polyester fibre. The ratlines are just 0.04mm in diameter and the mainstay 0.51mm. The model was carefully painted and given a patina to resemble the ship in service just before Nelson's chequer was applied. Mr Tsuboi was born in 1929 and is an active member of THE ROPE model building club in Tokyo, Japan.

VICTORY

SCRATCH-BUILT *VICTORY* 1:48 scale By KAZUNOBU SHIRAI

Given the large scale of this model, Mr Shirai was able to incorporate every detail possible. Planking of the hull and decks is authentic right down to plank length, the shift of the butts and trennel patterns. Each timber was cut and shaped from wood stock and then authentically scarphed together. The model was painted to capture her appearance in Portsmouth prior to 2015 in authentic colours.

Unfortunately, only the hull and portions of the masts were completed when Mr Shirai passed away from an illness. During his life he was a passionate model-

maker and a founding member of THE ROPE model club in Tokyo, Japan. He specialised in scale models of British and French warships of the eighteenth century and his works are a testament to the model-maker's art.

HELLER **HMS *VICTORY*** 1:100 scale

By DANIEL FISCHER

At the hands of Mr Daniel Fisher, Heller's kit becomes a masterpiece. Over the past decade, he has built, rebuilt, and reworked his model to incorporate the very latest research, improve scale fidelity and to add a full interior complete with ship's crew going about daily life. This inspirational model transports the viewer from our modern homes to the mess and gun decks of the eighteenth and nineteenth centuries.

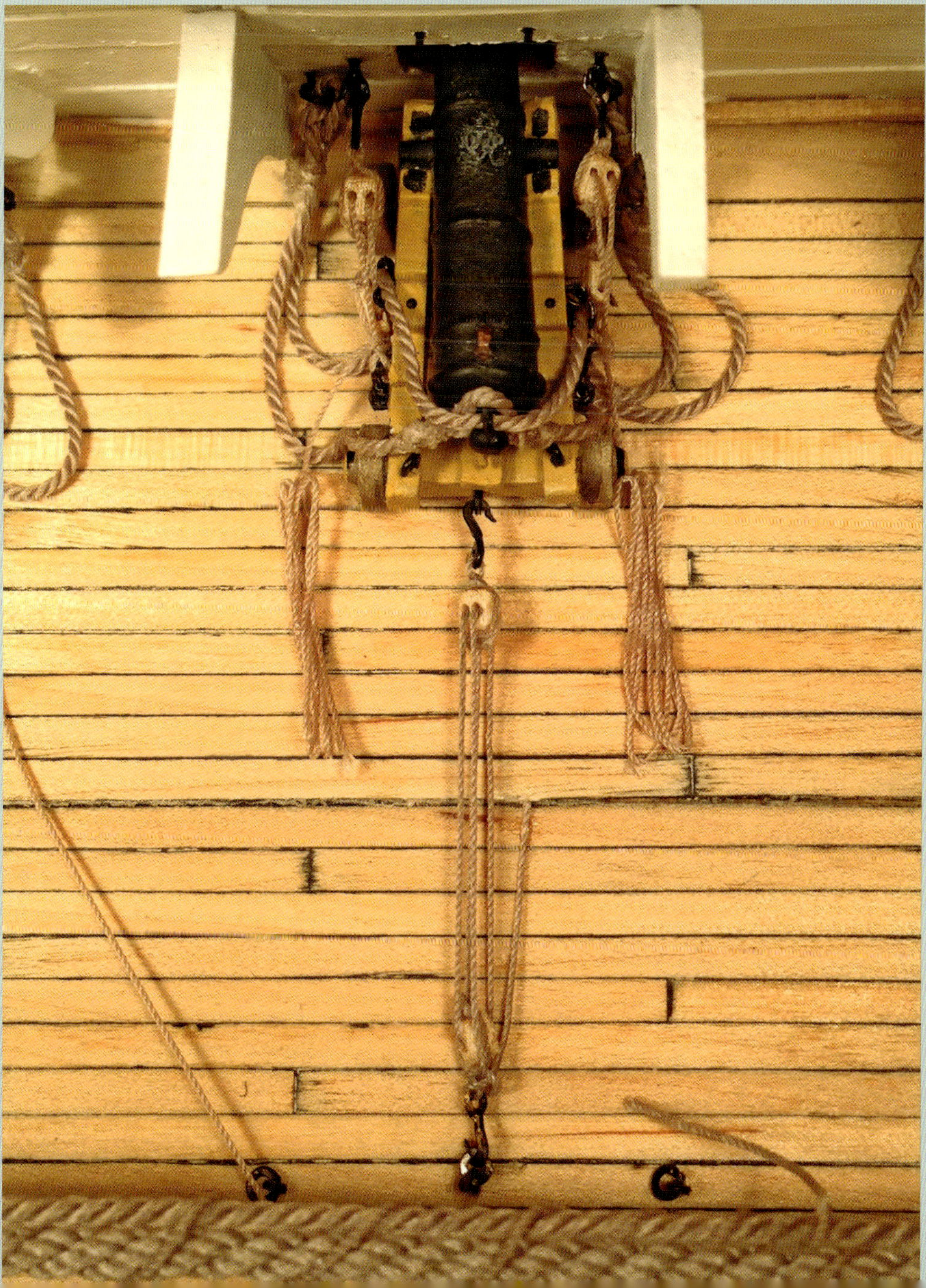

Appearance

By the time photography was invented in the 1830s, *Victory*'s active seagoing service was over and her appearance prior can only be deduced from ship's draughts, museum models, paintings, and written records (*eg*, Navy Board orders, carpenter's records, and memorials of events kept in a diary or letter). Individually, none of these are definitive. Orders were vague and captains were given considerable discretion, models were created for display purposes and might be decorated in the styles of the time or using inauthentic colours to highlight certain features of a proposed design or modification. The vibrancy of colour chosen by artists were selected to elicit specific emotions from their paintings, and not necessarily to portray the ship as she really was. Add to this the vagaries of time, memory and the construction of a ship by hand, all introduce variations from what was intended that conspires to confound the modern modelmaker. There may be no single piece of evidence that faithfully portrays the ship but when several are considered together we can piece together her probable appearance at a particular point in time.

VICTORY'S TOPSIDES AS DESIGNED AND COMMISSIONED (1759–1779)

Victory's designed appearance is illustrated by three draughts and several models. Draught J1849 (on page 2) is the original design draught but bear in mind that she was not fitted out immediately after her launch, which is shown on draught J8142 (page 3). Draught J8142 dates from the 1830s and is probably a copy or reconstruction of the lost 'as fitted' draught. It exists because of standing Navy Board instructions to produce and keep a record plan of all ships from about 1770. Draught J1850 (page 2) is a modern copy of the original sheer draught replacing the much damaged and difficult to read original plan. There are two undated slipway models of her original appearance, F5808 (below) and L2449 (page 49) that give a generally similar account, but these two models do differ in details. It is unclear if they are contemporary to *Victory*'s design and construction or not, although they are certainly not modern models.

What is notable about the slipway models is that they both include side entry ports on *both* sides of the ship. This is a departure from the usual practice of a single entry port on the starboard side. However, over her service, *Victory*'s progress books show that she received several repairs before her first commission so the portside one could have been closed off or converted into a gun port at some time prior to 1805. Model F2881 (page 50) supposedly representing *Victory*'s Trafalgar appearance shows gun ports instead of side entries on both sides. If *Victory* had a port-side entry, and when and if it was ever filled in remains a mystery. What is certain is that second one on the starboard side was *added* during her 1912 restoration to assist visitors moving in and out of the ship.

Another anomaly is that the three draughts do not show a mizzen stool for the backstays but they are present on the slipway models. The omission is odd because a stool is necessary given the

1:60 scale slipway model of *Victory*, F5808-001. A stern quarter view of the same model F5808-002 can be viewed on the Royal Museums Greenwich website in the Collections section. *(© National Maritime Museum, London F5808-001)*

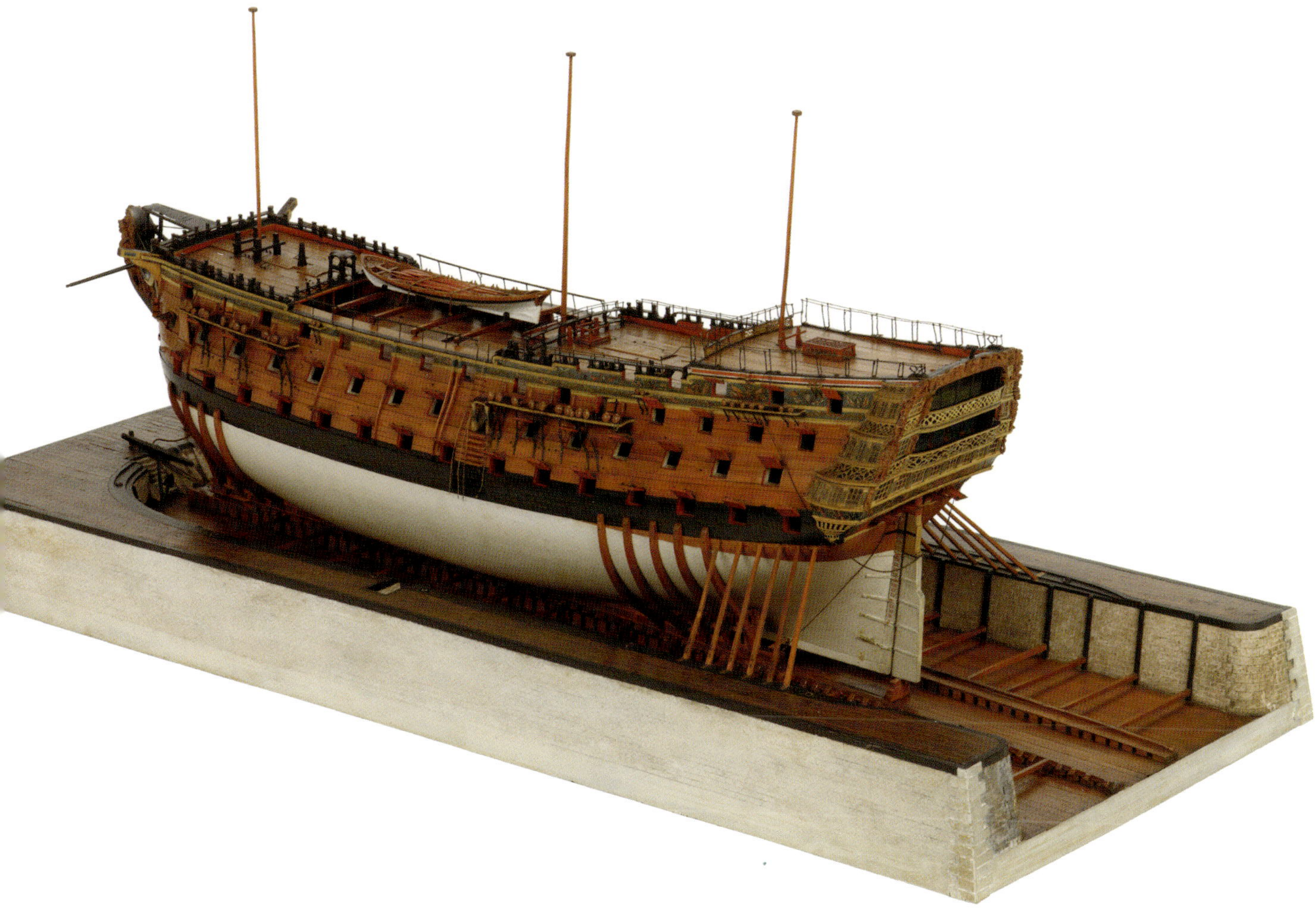

mizzen channel not being of sufficient length to accommodate an extra set of deadeyes for the backstays. A possible explanation is that because ships were rigged from experience and tradition, the draughtsman simply drew in channels and deadeyes as a placeholder, leaving it to the master rigger to install as he saw fit. By way of example, the number of *Victory*'s shroud deadeyes varied as circumstances and experience with the ship dictated:

	As Commissioned	*1803*	*As Restored*
Fore Mast	10	10	11
Main Mast	11	12	11
Mizzen Mast	7	7	6

Another area of difference is the carved work. Although the decorative work is illustrated on the 'as fitted' draught (J8142), it is different from the carved work shown on model L2449. The difference may illustrate that what is proposed on a draught is often different from what is actually fitted to the ship because carved work was approved by a separate commission and approval system.

It is instructive to compare *Victory* as restored to the draughts and models to help visualise the ship's appearance between then and now. In 1759 the lower gun deck had 15 gun ports compared to the restored ship which shows an additional one towards the bow. This extra port is a luff (bridle) port to assist in mooring and is not a gun port *per se*, although the port could have acted as a chase when necessary but guns were not allocated to them. The upper and middle gun decks of the 1759 draught show the same 15 gun ports. Although the gun port locations generally align, they do not do so precisely when comparing the 1759 draught to the restoration. For example, the foremost upper deck port on the restored ship is 14in aft of the location shown on the 1759 draught; and the 1759 draught shows the upper ports spaced 8ft 2in apart but the space between No 1 and No 2 ports is 9ft 9in. The source of the differences is unclear, perhaps draughting errors. In 1759 there were four stern gun ports that on the restored ship had been closed in and a single one cut in between the previous locations.

The fore and main channels on the restored ship are above the upper deck gun ports so the rigging no longer interferes with the guns, whereas on the 1759 draught they are below the gun ports reflecting the change ordered at her 1783–1784 refit. At this refit the forecastle was also lengthened and the run of the chains and chain plates differ. On the restored ship the channels are supported by iron brackets but on the draughts they

1:60 scale slipway model of *Victory*, F2449-003. Several close-up views of this model (L2449-001, L2449-005, L2449-006, L2449-007, L2449-009, L2449-010) can viewed on the Royal Museums Greenwich website in the Collections section, *(© National Maritime Museum, London F2449-003)*

are supported by wooden brackets fitted on their upper sides. The draughts show that the side ladder stops at the middle deck whereas they run to the top of the bulwarks on the restored ship. The two aftermost hull fenders did not change, but in 1759 there were two more fenders forward than on the restored vessel, and these may have evolved into the current chess tree for boat handling. The 1759 draught and slipway model show billboards (to protect the hull from the ends – 'bills' – of the anchor) but they were removed when the fore channels were raised and an anchor palm block fitted to the waist that is present on the restored ship for anchor stowage. The location of the wales, load water lines, plank sheer and upper work mouldings do not vary. *Victory* began a 'Middling Repair' in 1779 where she received copper sheathing to the under-water hull (completed in 1780), as in the restored ship. In 1788 *Victory*'s fore mast was moved aft by 2ft, the main mast by 1ft, and the mizzen by 6in to improve her sailing qualities based on her experience at sea; and in 1794 a flying jibboom added, and chain stoppers.

Inboard of the restored ship, both bitts and belfry were moved aft with the fore mast. The location of the galley stove chimney has not changed. Iron mast hoops replace rope woolding on masts. When built, *Victory* was fitted with four skid beams fitted to the waist, but these gradually became more substantial, fixed and eventually integrated with the decks either end of the waist as on the restoration. When commissioned, a lateen sail was carried at the mizzen but replaced with a quadrilateral 'spanker' during the 1800 refit.

The Prince of Wales feathers were taken from *Prince* (which was also at Trafalgar) and added to *Victory*'s stern in 1837. It is unknown what stern carvings *Victory* carried between 1800 and 1837. The central motif could have been a medallion featuring a bust of King George III, or his coat of arms, or a crown. It is known that a bust of Nelson was added after Trafalgar. The cannon and flags on either side of the central motif were thought to be present at Trafalgar.

THE 1800 'GREAT REPAIR' CHANGES TO TOPSIDES

Victory's 'Great Repair' most notably closed in her open stern and has defined the form of the ship until today. Comparison to the models and draughts illustrates changes to the number of windows, the number of lights per window, and if they were sashed or not. The form of the quarter galleries appears unchanged except that the top finishing was reduced to how it appears now. The height of the forecastle, quarter-deck, and poop deck bulwarks were ordered to become solid 'barricades', replacing the hammock netting. The evidence that 'barricades' were actually fitted come from models F2881 (below) and a half block model L0577 (page 51). Both models show barricades fitted to the forecastle and quarterdeck. However, the length of the quarter-deck barricade is shorter on F2881, where it begins at the end of the waist and extends to the break of the poop. A sketch by Turner (page 51) drawn after Trafalgar and before major repairs show that those on Model F2281 is the likely length. The location of the gun ports in the barricade varies between models. The block model L0577 is probably incorrect because the gun port spacing does not correspond to any other sources and the model may have been made as a mock up to illustrate the general nature of the alterations ordered. In contrast, the locations shown on model F2881 generally correspond with known locations of the gun ports and correspond to the location of frame timbers. The height

Contemporary model of *Victory* after the 1803 'Great Repair'. The gun port lids were later painted black to create the 'Nelson Chequer'. *(© National Maritime Museum, London F2881)*

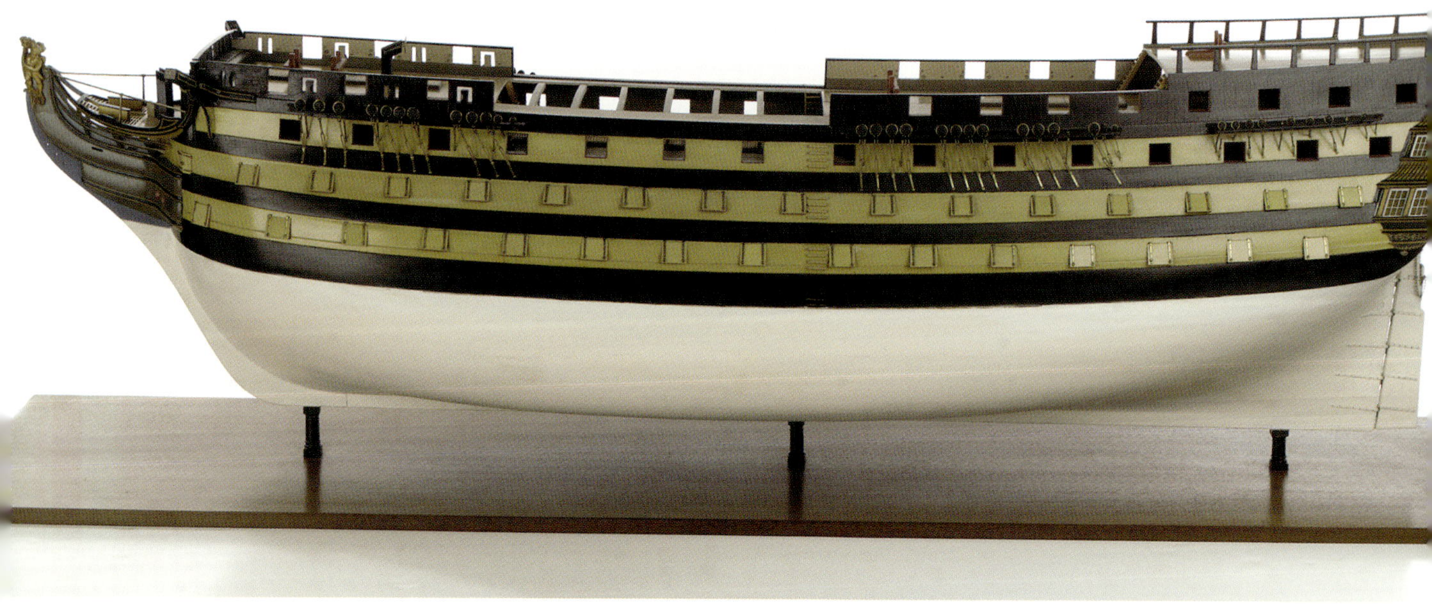

Block model L0577 of *Victory* with heightened bulwarks. *(© National Maritime Museum, London L0577)*

of the barricades appears to be determined by the height of the gun ports. These heightened bulwarks are not present on the restored ship and were probably removed after Trafalgar.

Poop barricades, although ordered, do not appear to have been fitted. Model F2881 shows open rails whereas Model L0577 simply shows nothing other than the low bulwark that is just over the height of the deck. The Turner sketch also shows no poop barricades. His sketch shows covered hammock cranes and netting suggesting that Model L0577 is correct for Trafalgar. As noted earlier, model F2881 also suggests that the side entry ports were not present at Trafalgar, but all sources, including L0577 show one on the starboard side. The Turner sketch is also interesting because it shows an open quarterdeck under the poop. The bulkheads would have been struck down for the battle and have not been replaced.

The restored ship does not carry the stern davits that were beginning to be fitted to ships in the fleet around 1800. Despite their general unpopularity, there is evidence that they were fitted at the *Victory*'s 1803 refit and present at Trafalgar judging from Clarkson Stansfield's painting of her being towed to Gibraltar after the battle (page 12).

J M W Turner's sketch of *Victory* after the battle and before repairs. *(© Tate Gallery D08275).*

This model shows the changes from *Victory*'s original square beakhead bulkhead (port side, L2626-001) to Sepping's round bow (starboard, L2626-002). The model also displays the change in typical colour schemes before and after the modification. *(© National Maritime Museum, London L2626-001 & L2626-002)*

1814–1816

Victory received a large repair at Portsmouth in which Seppings's reforms were adopted. This included a major alteration to a built-up 'round' bow that better protected against shot because it was essentially a continuation of the heavy hull side timbers; wooden knees were also replaced by iron. The difference between the bows is shown by Model L2626 (above). Quarter davits are present in two dated National Maritime Museum sketches of *Victory* in 1824 (PZ0907) and another dated 1827 (PZ0909) when she served as a guard ship and Port Admiral's flagship show the davits. However, a print by Cooke (page 53) does not show them but they could have been removed at that time at the captain's prerogative. During this time it was common practice for harbour service ships to have their masts and spars reduced in size. Photographs of the ship show this reduction that appears to cut down in size and length by about 10%.

1860

All the wales on *Victory* were removed and replaced with flush planking, glazed ports cut in below lower gun ports for ventilation, and the davits have reappeared for her role as a store ship. Many guns were removed and gun ports replaced with windows, and decoration reduced. During this period, the open canvas-covered hammock cranes were replaced with boarded up boxes to store hammocks. These boxes overhung the top of the waist outboard so as not to impinge on the walkways in the waist. These changes can be seen in McKenzie Thompson's watercolour (page13, dated roughly 1870–1890) and contemporary photographs on the Royal Museum Greenwich online archive of the ship at this time.

RESTORATION 1912 TO THE PRESENT

Victory's restoration as a museum ship was intended to bring her back to what was termed 'near Trafalgar' appearance. Notably, the round bow was removed and the original form restored. The details of restoration and decisions made are extensively covered in Arthur Bugler's (1966) two-volume *HMS Victory: Building, Restoration & Repair* and Alan McGowan's (1999) *HMS Victory: Her Construction, Career and Restoration.* Since her original restoration, changes are ongoing and ever evolving as research uncovers new details. The ship does not show forecastle or quarterdeck barricades thought to be present at Trafalgar.

VICTORY'S GENERAL PAINTWORK

The following notes rely heavily on the research in two scholarly papers published in *The Mariner's Mirror* entitled 'The Application and Scheme of Paintworks in British Men-of-War in the Late Eighteenth and Early Nineteenth Centuries' by Peter Goodwin published in 2013; and 'Pitch, Paint, Varnish and the Changing Colour Schemes of Royal Navy Warships, 1775–1815: A Summary of Existing Knowledge' by Brian Vale published in 2020. Both help determine *Victory*'s paintwork.

1765–1779

At her launch in 1765 and subsequent fitting out, *Victory*'s finish from the main wale to the down to the waterline was payed (*to cover it with a composition*) with waterproof applications of pitch and tar. Her hull sides were 'bright finished', being payed in a composition of pine varnish, turpentine and rosin that gives the ship's side a shiny light mahogany appearance. The area above this to the rails were payed with various types of varnish and/or oil paint made by mixing a coloured pigment with a binding agent such as linseed oil, thinning it with turpentine, and lead oxide to aid drying. This area was painted with a blue ground. Many Navy Board models of this period show a decorative frieze on top of the blue ground, but the frieze may just be a model-maker's whim and may not have been added to the actual ship. For example, Model L2449 shows a frieze painted on the blue background but not on Model F5808. Moreover, they do not always appear in paintings of ships from this time period either. An Admiralty order of 1715 noted that the sides of ships were to be 'painted of the usual colour yellow, and the ground black, and that both inside and out to be of a plain colour ... *except such parts of the head, stern and galleries as are usually friezed*.' [Quoted from Vale, B, article cited above. Note that all other quotations in this section are taken from this paper and primary sources are fully referenced there.] This early order explains at least where friezes were to be applied (and the ground was black not blue at this early period) and that ship's sides were painted yellow ochre. The yellow ochre was noted by the French Master Shipwright Blaise Ollivier's remarks on the painting of English ships in 1737. When *Victory* was built, the yellow paint specified had been replaced with varnish for better waterproof protection. Blaise Olliver's remarks support the change by noting that at this early period it was thought that paint encourages rot as moisture would get trapped between the wood and the paint.

When first commissioned, *Victory*'s name was painted in large letters across her stern, and this was ordered painted out by Admiral Keppel in 1776 for security reasons. She reacquired a painted name around 1781–1782 when his order was rescinded. The Navy Board seems to have had a standard style and typeface as shown on many 'as fitted' draughts of the 1770s and 1780s for reference.

With regards to *Victory*'s interior spaces, the officers' accommodations were probably

Victory in 1828. Hand-coloured print by E W Cooke. (*© National Maritime Museum, London PU5983*)

ARMAMENT CHANGES

Date	Gun Deck			Weather Deck	
	Lower	Middle	Upper	Quarter	Forecastle
May 1765	30 x 42pdr	28 x 24pdr	30 x 12pdr	10 x 6pdr	2 x 6pdr
February 1778	30 x 32pdr	28 x 24pdr	30 x 12pdr	10 x 12pdr	2 x 12pdr
July 1778	30 x 42pdr	28 x 24pdr	30 x 12pdr	10 x 12pdr	2 x 12pdr
March 1783	30 x 42pdr	28 x 24pdr	30 x 12pdr	10 x 12pdr	2 x 12pdr
October 1805	30 x 32pdr	28 x 24pdr	30 x 12pdr	12 x 12pdr 2 x 68pdr c	2 x 12pdr
March 1806	30 x 32pdr	28 x 24pdr	30 x12pdr	4 x 12pdr 8 x 32pdr c	2 x 32pdr c
November 1807*	28 x 32pdr	28 x 18pdr	30 x 12pdr	4 x 12pdr 8 x 32pdr c	2 x 32pdr c

Note: c = carronade; * *Victory* was formally reduced to a Second Rate of 98 guns. Although the total number of guns remained at 100, their weight was reduced. She was later re-rated as a First Rate with this armament because of a change to the ship ratings based on the number of gun decks (three) irrespective of the number of guns.

white because painting them any other colour (*eg*, green) required a special Board order. The bottom of the ship's boats were painted white by 1771 order. Contemporary models also show the inside face of the gun port lids and sills red ochre, and that the interior of some areas on models were red ochre or light blue (which could have been white that has discoloured over time). The bulwarks exposed to the weather were painted red ochre.

The advent of the War of American Independence (1777) made pitch, turpentine, and pine varnish expensive and by Navy Board order in 1778 the sides of ships were to be payed with a mixture of Stockholm tar and yellow or red ochre; and that the area from the wales to the waterline was to be treated with tallow and white lead. Shortly thereafter, in 1779, the Board ordered that black varnish should be used on mastheads and yards instead of tar, oil and blacking; and in 1780 it decided that it should also be used to waterproof the lower part of a ship's side from above the wales to the waterline.

1780

In 1780, the Navy Board established new norms for painting the exterior of ships. The order specified that the use of red ochre and Stockholm tar should cease and that the ship's sides should be painted in yellow above the main wale, the wale itself to the top of the copper painted black. The instruction also says 'as desired by the commander' allowing for some variation. The major painting works were carried out in the dockyard at refit and this order was applied to *Victory* in 1783. There was considerable variation noted in the use of yellow and black across the fleet with some ships having plain yellow sides to black streaks depending on the captain's preference, or in some cases the black was used to help camouflage by making it appear smaller or larger.

1783–1794

At this time we get a clear idea of the *shade* of yellow and the use of other colours on a ship. The yellow ochre provided to the ships was dark and needed to be lightened as noted by the Navy Board, '... unless the captain of a private ship will pay the [dockyard] painters for additional white to be mixed with the yellow, it is so very dark a colour that it makes the ship look very dirty and dismal.' A general ship painting contract from 1785 with Thomas Winsloe of Yelverton lists ten pigments: Venetian red, vermilion, red lead, Spanish brown, stone ochre, umber, blue black, verdigris, Prussian blue and white lead. This contract made it clear that the colours were not to be laid on pure but mixed as follows:

- *Yellow Colour: To be made of the best sort of Spruce Oaker (sic). One hundredweight of it to be mixed with half a hundredweight of the best white lead, exclusive of any Whiting, or any other alloy and the said ingredients to be mixed as to produce the most agreeable Yellow Colour.*
- *Port Red Colour: To be of a mixture of five pounds weight of the best Red lead with half a pound weight of the best Venetian red; the latter to keep the Colour from flying off.*
- *Red Colour: To be the best Venetian Red, with no other mixture but that of a little Red lead to heighten and dry it.*
- *Stone Colour: To be of the best White lead and Umber.*

The specified mix would have produced a light yellow colour, which is corroborated by observations made by Colonel Walter Fawkes at the Battle of Nile in 1798. He noted that the majority of the British ships had their broadsides painted a *light yellow* whereas the French vessels were predominantly dark yellow. He makes no mention of gun port lid colours, confirming that the outer faces of the lids at this time were likely painted in the same colour as the broadsides creating an unbroken yellow band (or hull) from stem to stern when the ports were closed.

Port red, red colour, and stone appear to be used in the interior walls and bulwarks. Red was certainly used on the inside surfaces of the gun port lids because the Winsloe contract specified they should be painted in 'port red' (a dark red like port wine?), and specified: 'Red colour: usually painted under the Main Decks, Quarter Decks, Fore Castle, Weather Works (*eg*, inner bulwarks exposed to the weather) and the Wastes etc. To be of the best Venetian red, with no other mixture, but that of a little Red lead to heighten and dry it.' Interestingly, the contract *does not* instruct the use of red on all interior sides and bulwarks of the lower decks or the areas below the waterline, such as the orlop, the store rooms, the hold and the cockpit, which were probably painted white (or a light colour) to optimise light levels. Although red was officially replaced by light yellow in 1807, no evidence has come to light indicating exactly when the *Victory* changed her red-painted inboard weather works to yellow. Gun carriages were supplied by the Ordnance Board painted red ochre, but they were often repainted yellow after embarkation.

In 1778, the Navy Board ordered that new ships and those preparing for sea should have their between decks white-washed. Whitewashing is not a synonym for painting white as used in modern English. Whitewash is a specific compound made from a quick lime base with the addition of fish glue to give adhesion to bare wood to cleanse the interior of ships following an outbreak of disease, and was thought to prevent future infection. Sir Roger Curtis, wrote that 'as a preventative against sickness, as well as when contagion rages, the whitewashing of the interior parts of the ship twice or thrice a year would, by removing noxious effluvia, greatly contribute to the health of the people.' Thomas Trotter, Physician of the Fleet, wrote: 'Whitewashing, at all times delicate and cleansing ... excites ideas of personal cleanliness among the people. But it may justly be reckoned a purifier of the atmosphere: quick lime strongly attracts the fixed air of the well or hold and also nitrous air which some physicians assert is contagion itself.'

1800–1803

Victory's 'Great Repair' occurred in the dockyard and the painting orders in place would have been followed. The hull would remain yellow ochre but all wales painted black. Gun port lid exteriors remained yellow ochre. Although the *Victory* could have adopted whitewash or yellow ochre for her interior spaces at any time between early 1803 and 1805, the change most likely occurred when Thomas Hardy superseded Samuel Sutton as Captain. By 1805 *Victory*'s interior was certainly white. The *Victory*'s carpenter on 18 August 1805 recorded: 'To whitewashing the Tiers, Wings Cock-pits Store-roomes (*sic*) Lower & Middle Decks – Lime 12 Bushels Glue 12 Pounds.'

1803–1805

Under Lord Nelson's command *Victory* took on her most famous appearance. It is recorded that he preferred a very light shade of yellow for *Victory*'s sides and proposed that private ships in the fleet be painted a light yellow mixed in a 6lbs white to 1lb yellow ochre ratio. The Board of Admiralty rejected his proposal and September 1805 records show that *Victory* was applying a 1 yellow to 1.3 white mix.

The carpenter's entry dated 14 September 1805 provides some insight into *Victory*'s external and interior colour: 'To painting the ship's side after caulking, the Gunroom and Officers Apartments under the Awning and Quarter deck Waist &c. after Refitting and the paint and materials consumed for the above entry listed in the margin are given as: Yellow – 350lbs; Black – 150lbs; White – 450lbs.; Oil – 47 gallons; Brushes – 20 in No.' This record also suggests that the yellow could also have been employed to cover the exposed faces of the cabin bulkheads for the master and secretary, and the forward face of the captain's dining cabin under the poop, as these bulkheads were exposed to the elements and needed protection. This is in stark contrast to the ship as originally restored that had these areas panelled in dark stained wood. In 2015 the bulkheads under the poop were repainted the same terracotta ochre colour as the hull.

The date of the adoption of the 'Nelson Chequer' is unknown. It involved painting, on top of the yellow hulls, black strakes which ran the length of the ship between the gun decks – one strake in the case of a 74, and two for First Rates – with the outside surfaces of the gun port lids painted black. It is known that the mobilisation of the fleet after the failure of the Treaty of Amiens in 1803 saw the ships of the Mediterranean Fleet adopt the colour schemes preferred by Lord Nelson. There was precedent for this practice because the ships of Nelson's 1798 squadron were painted in identical fashion to provide some distinguishing features from the enemy. When new ships joined Nelson's fleet, they also emulated his style and all of these changes were not paid for or applied by the dockyards, but had to be paid for by the ship's captains themselves as documented in several letters to family members complaining about the cost or noting it as something remarkable. The lower masts were painted ochre, while tops, mastheads, cross-trees and caps and lower yards were painted black. The uppermost yards were probably treated with black varnish.

Up until this point the term 'light yellow' or 'yellow ochre' meant the paint had a distinctly yellow cast. However, archaeological research on *Victory* suggests that in 1805 the yellow had a distinct pink or 'terracotta' cast. This work scrutinised *rase marks* – marks cut into timber that include the date at which the timber entered the yard, or was converted into parts of the ship. These marks were cross-referenced against the layers of paint found on the timbers and the dates of *Victory*'s repairs to allow an identification of the paint colour at a specific time. The accuracy of dating was improved by studying the layers of dirt between each layer of paint. When the ship is laid up the layers of dirt are thin but when at sea they are thick, and when several coats of paint have been applied in short succession, dirt layers do not exist.

Given this new evidence, where did the pink tone come from? One theory is that the pink tone was the result of mixing some surplus of red paint noted in her carpenter's accounts from 1805 to the yellow and black mixes giving the yellow a pinkish cast and turning black to an off-black. An alternative theory is that because ochre is a naturally occurring product, it could vary in colour depending on where it was mined or processed, and the pigments issued to *Victory* at this time may have had a red undertone that turned pink with the addition of white lead.

The Carpenter's expenses for September 1805 also showed that the ship's boats (the barge, launch, three yawls and pinnace) were painted white, black and 'yellow'. This probably applied to all boats except the Admiral's barge in which the inboard works and wash strake were probably green because this colour was associated with flag ranks. The amount of green (verdigris) in the Carpenter's store was small so unlikely to be used on any other boats.

With regards to the flags flown by *Victory* at Trafalgar, artist's depictions vary. Based on written eyewitness accounts and orders, *Victory* flew the following flags at the battle: White Ensign at the mizzen ensign halyard; Union Flag at the main topgallant (some artists erroneously show a White Ensign); St George's Cross at the fore topgallant; Union Flag on the fore jibstay. Signals (*eg*, 'England expects...' were hoisted at the mizzen in twelve separate hoists), with final signal '1-6' ordered raised at the main topgallant where it stayed until shot away.

1814–1816

Victory received a large repair at Portsmouth in which Seppings's reforms were adopted. The ship was repainted and the yellow replaced by white. The gun port lids remained black. Ships in commission were painted with double strakes along the gun ports, but only one line when in ordinary. *Victory* retained double strakes in deference to Nelson.

1860

All the wales on *Victory* were removed and replaced with flush planking. Name on stern in small letters painted white in a cartouche.

1912 – 2015

In 1910, the Society for Nautical Research began work to return the ship to what was described as a 'near Trafalgar' appearance. During the 1922–1927 restoration it was believed that *Victory*'s sides were painted 'bright' yellow and chrome yellow paint was used. Since then, the hull has been repainted using different commercially available paints whose tone became progressively darker, but the colours were not based on archival evidence. Moreover, in the 1980s, despite the evidence that *Victory*'s internal colour scheme was white, a dark wood stain and varnish was used to refinish various officers' cabins as noted earlier.

2015 to the present

In 2016 *Victory* was repainted in the terracotta shade archaeological evidence suggested. Her name was written large across her transom in white. Weather works painted in the terracotta ochre replacing the dark varnished wood.

Victory's stern as restored in 2015. *(Author's collection)*

As commissioned (1776), outboard profile. Carving and decoration detail omitted for clarity. Decoration details can be found on Model L2449 viewable in the Royal Museum Greenwich on-line archive. This model shows painted friezes on the blue background that may not have appeared on the actual ship as shown by Model F5808.

As commissioned (1776), stern. Details of possible carving and decoration detail can be found on Model L2449-10. The details differ from Model F5808. Carving and decoration detail omitted for clarity but the relevant area is rendered in the colour of the decoration. *(All drawings by John McKay)*

As commissioned (1776), head rails. The figurehead as commissioned can be found on Model L2400-1 and L2400-2. Carving and decoration detail omitted for clarity.

As commissioned (1776), quarter galleries. Detail taken from Model L2449.

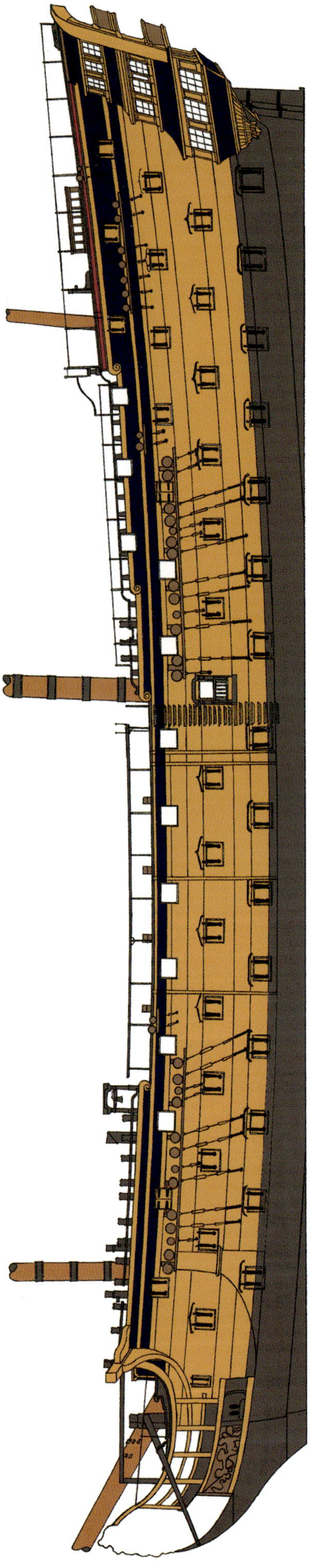

Outboard profile, 1783. Colour scheme reconstructed from Navy Board instructions. Carving and decoration detail omitted for clarity.

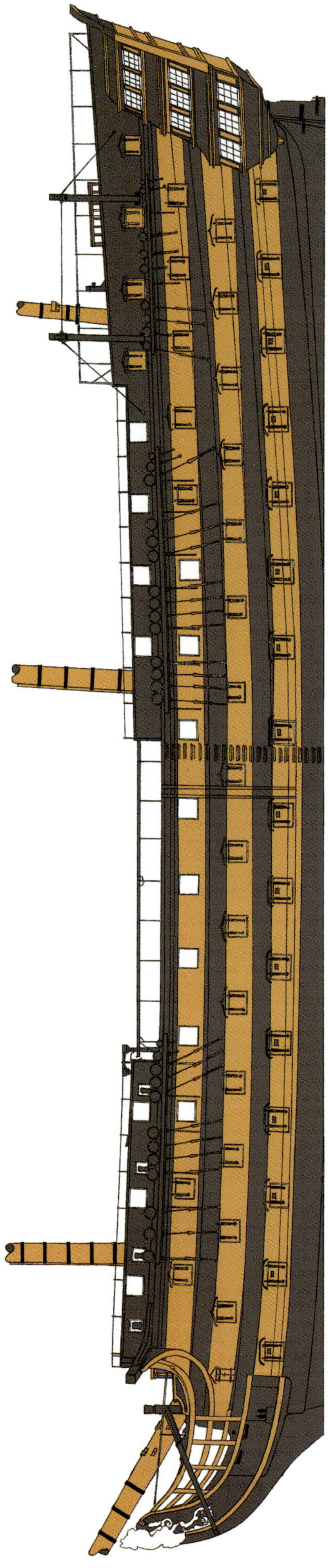

Outboard profile, 1803. Colour scheme reconstructed from Navy Board instructions. Carving and decoration detail omitted for clarity.

Outboard profile, 1805. *Victory* in the 'Nelson Chequer' and in the terracotta shade of ochre discovered through archaeological research by the *HMS Victory* museum. Forecastle and quarterdeck bulwarks are shown raised as per Navy Board order. The heightened poop bulwarks do not appear to have been fitted, based on J M W Turner's sketch (page 52) of this area after the battle but before major repairs. This profile shows the probable appearance of the ship at Trafalgar. Carving and decoration detail omitted for clarity.

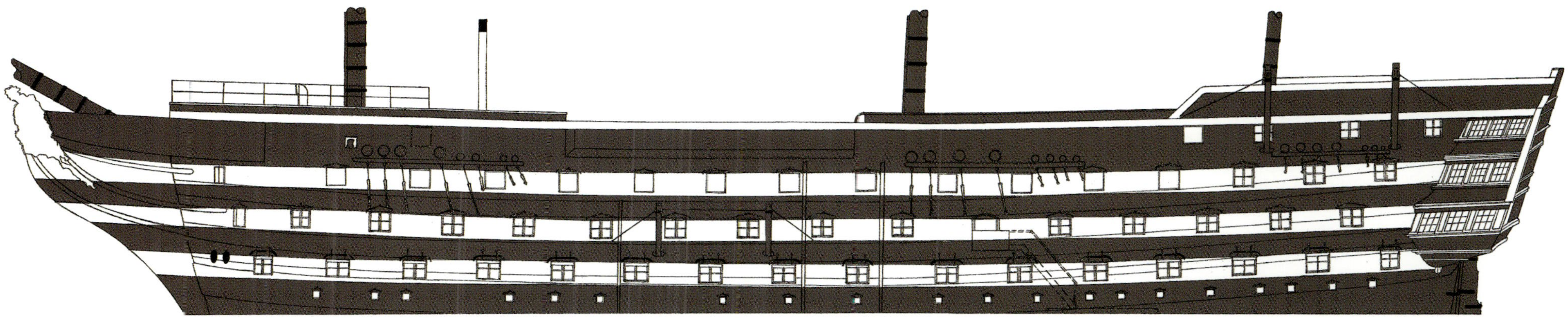

Outboard profile, late nineteenth century. Seppings's reforms and her conversion to a store or Port Admiral's ship greatly altered the profile of the ship. Carving and decoration detail omitted for clarity.

Stern, 1783. Colour scheme reconstructed from Navy Board instructions. Carving and decoration as per Model L2449 or F5808. Carving and decoration detail omitted for clarity.

Stern, 1803. Colour scheme reconstructed from Navy Board instructions. Details of stern carving and decoration is generally unknown. Carving and decoration detail omitted for clarity.

Stern, 1805. The details of the stern carvings are omitted because it is not certain what they were at this time. There is evidence that the spray of flags at the taffrail was present at Trafalgar. The central motif may have been a bust of George III.

Stern, late nineteenth century. The stern decoration was much reduced; Prince of Wales Feathers were added in 1837, and her name in a small oval cartouche. Some decoration detail has been omitted for clarity. Details of the decoration can be found on photographs of the stern at the National Maritime Museum Greenwich's online archive.

Port-side cutboard profile, as first restored. The ship as restored to 'near Trafalgar' appearance. The colours chosen were not based on archival evidence. This profile of the port side shows a side entry port added. Arthur Bugler's book provides a detailed reference as to the decisions made at the time of the restoration. Carving and decoration detail omitted for clarity.

Starboard-side outboard profile, as first restored. It does not show a side entry port which was not present when originally restored. Carving and decoration detail omitted for clarity.

Stern, as first restored. It is unclear which of the existing decorations were carried by the ship when her stern was closed in during her 'Great Repair' of 1800–1803 and the decoration present today may have been added any time during her long career. The details of her decoration and colour details are readily viewed on the restored ship in Portsmouth.

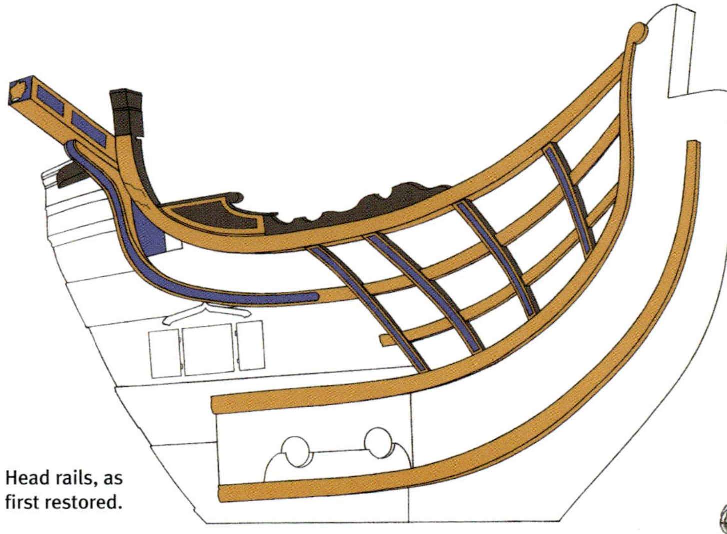

Head rails, as first restored.

Quarter galleries, as first restored.

Figurehead, as currently restored.

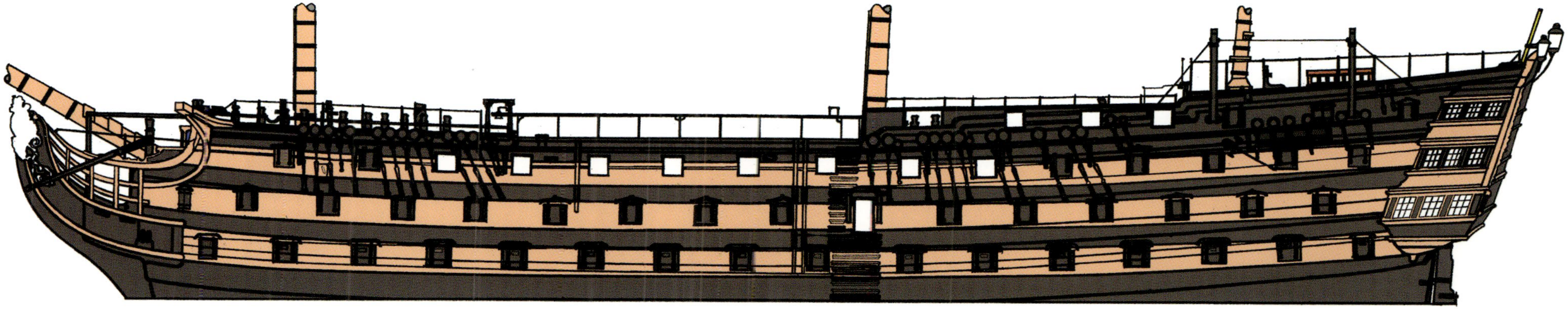

Port-side outboard profile, as currently restored. The ship was repainted in 2015 to reflect her true colours at Trafalgar based on the latest archaeological research. At present the restored ship has not been fitted with heightened bulwarks. Carving and decoration detail omitted for clarity but is the same as when the ship was originally restored.

Stern, as currently restored.

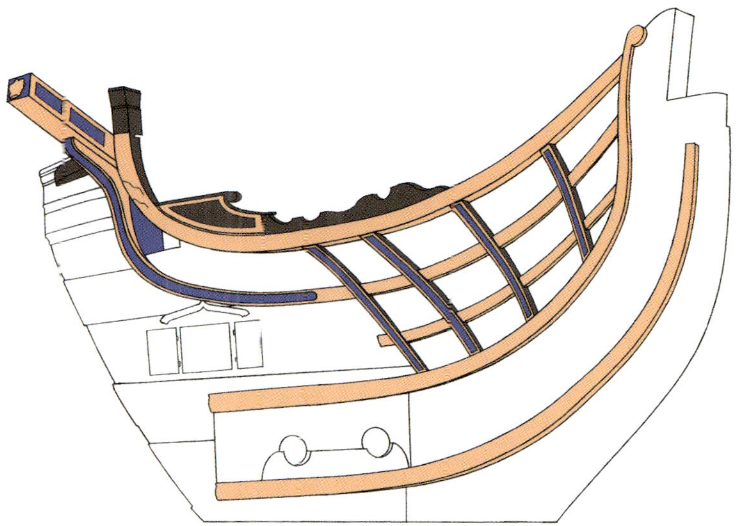

Head rails, as currently restored.

Quarter galleries, as currently restored. The decorations and details of the stern omitted for clarity. The details of the decoration and colour details are as on the restored ship at Portsmouth.

Selected References

BIBLIOGRAPHY

Adkins, R, *Nelson's Trafalgar* (Viking Penguin, New York 2004).

Bugler, A, *HMS Victory: Building, Restoration & Repair* (HMSO, London 1966).

Eastland, J & Ballantyne, I, *Seaforth Historic Ships: HMS Victory* (Seaforth Publishing, Barnsley 2005).

Goodwin, P G, *HMS Victory. Owner's Workshop Manual* (Haynes, Sparkford 2012).

Goodwin, P G, 'The Application and Scheme of Paintworks in British Men-of-War in the Late Eighteenth and Early Nineteenth Centuries', *The Mariner's Mirror* 99(3), (2013), 287-300. DOI: 10.1080/00253359.2013.815993

Granier, H, *Histoire des marins français (1789–1815)* (Marines éditions, Nantes 1998).

Hackney, N C L, *HMS Victory* (Patrick Stephens, London 1970).

Howarth, D, *Trafalgar. The Nelson Touch* (Fontana, Glasgow 1971).

Jang, Kerry, *Ships Models from the Age of Sail: Building and Enhancing Commercial Kits* (Seaforth Publishing, Barnsley 2022).

Longridge, C N, *The Anatomy of Nelson's Ships* (Naval Institute Press, Annapolis, 10th impression 1987).

McGowan, A, *HMS Victory: Her Construction, Career, and Restoration* (Chatham Publishing, London 1999).

McKay, J, *Anatomy of the Ship: The 100-gun Ship Victory* (Conway Maritime Press, London 1987).

Petersson, L, *Rigging Period Ship Models* (Chatham Publishing, London 2000).

Roberts, D H (ed), *18th Century Shipbuilding: Remarks on the navies of the English and Dutch by Blaise Ollivier (1737)* (Jean Boudriot, Paris 1992).

Vale, B, 'Pitch, Paint, Varnish and the Changing Colour Schemes of Royal Navy Warships, 1775–1815: A summary of existing knowledge', *The Mariner's Mirror*, 106(1), (2020) 30-42. DOI: 10.1080/00253359.2020.1712841

Reed, P, *Modelling Sailing Men-of-War* (Chatham Publishing, London 2000).

Reed, P, *Period Ship Modelmaking: An Illustrated Masterclass* (Seaforth Publishing, Barnsley 2007).

INTERNET RESOURCES

Research

Royal Museums Greenwich (National Maritime Museum) archives https://www.rmg.co.uk/collections

Nautical Research Guild https://www.thenrg.org/

Model Ship World https://modelshipworld.com/

The Rope https://theropetokyo-en.jimdofree.com/

Accessories and Kits

HiS Model https://www.hismodel.com/

Vanguard Models (A source of fittings and rigging blocks) https://vanguardmodels.co.uk/

Caldercraft. A detailed build log of this kit by the manufacturer. http://www.jotika-ltd.com/Pages/1024768/Victory_Front.htm

Jotika http://jotika-ltd.com/Pages/1024768/PSA_Paint.htm

Scale Warship https://scalewarship.com/ sailing-ships/hms-victory

Navy Models and Books https://navy modelsand-books.co.uk/shop/meridian-1700-scale-trafalgar-ships/british/ mt1-hms-victory/

GHQ https://www.ghqmodels.com/products/100-gun-ship-of-the-line-hms-victory-full-sails

Dafinsmus http://www.dafinismus.de/ index_en.html

Langton Miniatures http://www.rodlangton.com/napoleonic/list.htm

Warlord Games Black Seas https://www.warlordgames.com/ black-seas-hms-victory/

Henry Turner https://wargaming3d. com/product/gb-pre-reconstruction-hms-victory-104-guns-1765-1800/

Scaledecks https://scaledecks.com/

Artist Hobby. These kits are available from on-line auction sites or some model shops such as Hobby Search. https://www.1999.co.jp/eng/10707626

General Model Shops

Cornwall Model Boats https://www.cornwallmodelboats.co.uk/index.html

Hannants https://www.hannants.co.uk/